T0104967

Simple Devotions: God's Daily Blessings

(For Very Young Children)

Dr. John Thomas Wylie

authorHOUSE®

AuthorHouse™
1663 Liberty Drive
Bloomington, IN 47403
www.authorhouse.com
Phone: 1 (800) 839-8640

Published by AuthorHouse 02/08/2018

ISBN: 978-1-5462-2832-5 (sc)
ISBN: 978-1-5462-2831-8 (e)

Print information available on the last page.

Contents

A Word To Parents

Like most parents, you will likely do all that you can do to create solid, cheerful christian kids – who will end up plainly sound, upbeat christian grown-ups. What's more, Simple Devotions: God's Daily Blessings can offer assistance.

Every day highlights a Biblical guarantee or truth, a short reverential in view of an age – fitting subject, and an eccentric rhyme catching the day's reality with happy appeal. The endearing messages made by the creator are carefully fit to draw in even the most youthful youngster and joy you, a parent, as well!

Basic Devotions Every Day Little Blessings is an exuberant experience – a stroll through the sacred writings where youthful kids can find for themselves god's identity, his many guarantees, and how those guarantees identify with us during circumstances such as the present.

This publication is the perfect way to introduce children to the joy of having some special time with God every day.

Dr. Wylie urges parents to read with their children and also interpret words and scripture they may not understand. All scripture is of the King James Version unless otherwise indicated.

Reverend Dr. John Thomas Wylie

Day 1
God's Favorite Creation

(In the beginning God created the heaven and the earth. Genesis 1:1)

Do you get a kick out of the chance to play with mud or work with pieces? Is it accurate to say that it isn't enjoyable to make clever shapes and tall towers?

Envision how much fun God had making fish and mountains and stars and waterways! God made everything from the moon high in the sky to the wiggly worms somewhere down in the ground. Yet, his most loved making of all is YOU!

God made all that I can see, And the best part is that he made me!

Day 2
Look – Alikes

(So God created man in his own image, in the image of God created he him; male and female created he them Genesis 1:27)

God made loads of various types of individuals! We come in all shapes and sizes and hues. Indeed, even in your own particular family, no one appears to be identical. Yet, regardless of how diverse we look, we are all piece of God's family.

Of the considerable number of things God made when he made the world, individuals are the most exceptional!

God made everybody, both you and me. We are all piece of his family.

Day 3
Wild Things

(And God made the beast of the earth after his kind, and cattle after their kind, and every thing that creepeth upon the earth after his kind: and God saw that it was good. Genesis 1:25)

Whenever you go for a stroll in the forested areas of travel to the zoo, perceive what number of various types of creatures you can discover. There are deer and dragonflies, lion and panthers, seals and snakes – and that is quite recently the start! There are a greater number of creatures on the planet than could fit in one place. What's more, God made each and every one of them. On the off chance that he can make bears and bugs, there's nothing he can't do.

God made the greater part of the winged animals that take off, God made the lions that thunder!

Day 4
Fantastic You

(And God saw every thing that he had made, and, behold, it was very good Genesis 1:31).

Have you at any point felt like no one prefers you? We as a whole have days when we feel disregarded or singled out or left out. In any case, do you know who thinks' identity stunning each and every moment of each and every day? God does! After God completed the process of making everything on the planet, he looked it over and preferred what he saw. Whenever you feel like no one enjoys you, recall that God supposes you're awesome!

At the point when God takes a gander at me, He loves what he sees.

Day 5
The Rainbow Promise

(I do set my bow in the cloud, and it shall be for token of a covenant between me and the earth Genesis 9:13)

Where did rainbows originate from? Quite a while back, a major flood secured the entire earth with water; After the flood, God put an excellent rainbow in the sky as a guarantee to individuals that there could never be a flood like that again. Each rainbow is an exceptional indication of God's affection for us.

God sent us a rainbow to indicate us he wants to think about it (he cares). At whatever point we see one, we realize that he's there.

Day 6
All We Need

(That in blessing I will bless thee, and in multiplying I will multiply thy seed as the stars of the heaven, and as the sand which is upon the sea shore; and they seed shall possess the gate of his enemies; And in thy seed shall all the nations of the earth be blessed; because thou hast obeyed my voice Genesis 17,18)

Have you at any point asked your mother or father to purchase something at the store? Now and again we think we require more than what we have. Be that as it may, God truly has given every one of us sorts of awesome things. We have families who adore us, companions to play with, sustenance to eat, and houses to keep us sheltered and warm. That is a considerable measure to be glad about and grateful for!

Enable me to be upbeat (be happy) for all that you give, Family and companions and a protected place to live.

Day 7
Don't Be Shy (Timid)

(Now therefore go, and I will be with thy mouth, and teach thee what thou shalt say Exodus 4:12)

Do you ever feel so bashful that you can't let out the slightest peep? Particularly around individuals you don't have a clue? When you meet another person, recall that God will enable you to talk up. You don't need to stress over what to state. Simply grin (smile) your greatest grin and make proper acquaintance. Before you know it, you won't feel timid any longer!

When I feel timid, I have nothing to state, But God encourages me talk in my own particular manner!

Day 8
"Never Stop Praying."

(1 Thessalonians 5:17)

Pray constantly in light of the fact that God cherishes for you to converse with Him, and He is dependably listening.

Do This: Talk to God all as the day progressed.

Day 9
"Shout To The Lord."

(Psalm 100:1)

Hop! Holler! Shout! – Yell! We have something incredible to tell! Our God is superb! Do This: As uproarious as you can, yell, "God is awesome"

Do This: As Loud as you can, shout, "God is Wonderful, God is Awesome!"

Day 10
Thanks, Mom And Dad

(Honor your dad and mom Exodus 20:12)

Your folks do a wide range of pleasant things for you. They take great care of you. They buckle down so you'll have all that you require. They read to you and show you new things. You can demonstrate them you cherish them by doing pleasant things for them as well. You can hear them out, do what they ask without griping, and enable them all you to can. What's more, giving them an embrace is an awesome approach to express profound gratitude! A debt of gratitude is in order for my folks – a blessing from above. Help me to give them the greater part of my adoration.

Day 11
A Letter From God

(Therefore shall ye lay up these my words in your heart and in your soul, and bind them for a sign upon your hand, that they may be as frontlets between your eyes Deuteronomy 11:18).

The Bible resembles an awesome huge letter from God. A Love letter. In the Bible God reveals to all of us the critical things he need us to know. He enlightens us regarding himself. He discloses to us how to tail him and the amount he cherishes us. The majority of all, he informs us concerning his Son, Jesus. It's enjoyable to peruse the Bible – it resembles perusing a letter from your absolute best companion.

The Bible is God's extraordinary love letter to me. It causes me to see all he needs me to be.

Day 12
Only God

(There is none like unto the God of Jeshurun, who rideth upon the heaven in thy help, and in his excellency on the sky. Deuteronomy 33:26)

Think quick! Do you know any individual who can make a sea? Or, on the other hand make the sun? Or, then again manufacture a man out of clean? All things considered, God can. He can do anything. The best part is that God guarantees to deal with us perpetually, Isn't it incredible to have somebody so magnificent and intense looking out for us?

You make the world, both the land and the sea, And you guarantee dependably to deal with me.

Day 13
"Give Thanks Whatever Happens"

(In every thing give thanks: for this is the will of God in Christ Jesus concerning you. 1 Thessalonians 5:18)

Be Thankful constantly. In great circumstances or terrible circumstances, be grateful for all that you have.

Do This: Say "thank you" to the individual reading to you."

Day 14
Safe And Sound

(The eternal God is thy refuge, and underneath are the everlasting arms; and he shall thrust out the enemy from before thee; and shall say, Destroy them. Deuteronomy 33:27).

What do you do when you're terrified? Do you hole up behind your father or your mother? Do you hurried to your room or draw a cover over your head? Those things can enable you to feel safe, But notwithstanding when your folks aren't anywhere in the vicinity or you can't discover a place to cover up, recollect God can do anything. Also, he guarantees to dependably protect you.

When I get terrified, I know God is there. He guards me in his cherishing care.

Day 15
"God Is Love"

(And we have known and believed the love that God hath to us. God is love; and he that dwelleth in love dwelleth in God, and God in him. 1 John 4:16)

God is patient and kind. You can be as well!

Do This: Act like God today by being adoring and kind to others.

Day 16
God Is There

(There shall not any man be able to stand before thee all the days of thy life; as I was with Moses, so I will be with thee: I will not fail thee, nor forsake thee. Joshua 1:5)

The Bible is loaded with stories about individuals doing astonishing things. Take Joshua, for example. God requesting that he lead a tremendous gathering of individuals into an obscure place. Really alarming, huh? However, God guaranteed Joshua that he'd deal with him and help him consistently. What's more, God did quite recently that!

God is with me wherever I go. I know it's valid. He reveals to me so.

Day 17
A Solid Rock

(There is none holy as the Lord: for there is none beside thee: neither is there any rock like our God. 1 Samuel 2:2)

Do you jump at the chance to gather rocks? Rocks come in every single distinctive size, and they're quite astounding. Have you at any point attempted to break one? They're truly solid. Enormous rocks are extraordinary to remain on when you need to see higher or sit on when you have to rest. That is the reason the Bible calls God a stone. God is unfathomably solid, and he's dependably there when we require him. Really astonishing!

God is our Rock. He's strong and solid. At whatever point we believe Him, we'll never turn out badly.

Day 18
"Do Not Lie To Each Other"

(Lie not one to another, seeing that ye have put off the old man with his deeds. Colossians 3:9)

Telling untruths (Lies) resembles tossing mud on a perfect divider. Yuck! It makes a major, enormous wreckage of things. God needs us to dependably come clean. Continuously

Do This: Be straightforward. Try not to advise misleads cause somebody harm or to get yourself out of inconvenience.

Day 19
Forgive Each Other"

(Forbearing one another, and forgiving one another, if any man have a quarrel against any: even as Christ forgave you, so also do ye. Colossians 3:13)

Once in a while companions hurt our emotions. Now and then our sibling or sister makes us frantic. Excusing them rapidly and full is the best approach to get ideal back to GLAD and HAPPY.

Do This: Forgive the individuals who hurt or baffle you today!

Day 20
Children, Obey Your Parents

(Children, obey your parents in all things: for this is well pleasing unto the Lord. Colossians 3:20)

Do What your mama and daddy say. Comply, obey them consistently.

Do This: Smile and say, "Truly, Mommy or Yes daddy," when you are inquired to accomplish something today.

Day 21
Help Those Who Are Weak

(Now we exhort you, brethren, warn them that are unruly, confort the feebleminded, support the weak, be patient toward all men 1 Thessalonians 5:14)

Be a helper. This makes God smile. Do This: Help by putting your things away after you use them today.

Day 22
Peekaboo

(But the Lord said unto Samuel, Look not on his coountenance, or on the height of his stature because I have refused him; for the Lord seeth not as man seeth; for man looketh on the outward appearance, but the LORD looketh on the heart. 1 Samuel 16:7)

What's the main thing individuals see when they take a gander at you? Your spots? Your hair? Your enormous grin? Whatever individuals see when they take a gander at you, it's just a little bit of what makes you. Be that as it may, when God takes a gander at you, he sees every little thing about you, similar to how amicable or keen or kind you are. The vast majority of all, God sees the brilliant individual he has made. What's more, that is the thing that he adores most.

God sees inside me, he finds in my heart. To him I am superb, exquisite, furthermore, keen!

Day 23
A Bright Light

(For thou art my lamp, O Lord; and the LORD will lighten my darkness 2 Samuel 22:29)

Today around late evening time, ask you mother or father to turn out every one of the lights in your room. It gets exceptionally dull, isn't that right? At that point request that they walk out on. What happens now? Your room is loaded with light once more. That is the thing that God resembles. Simply knowing God cherishes us makes our entire world splendid. God's adoration is so splendid, It can illuminate the night! He helps up your general surroundings!

Day 24
"Do Everything Without Complaining"

(Do all things without murmurings and disputings: Philippians 2:14)

Try not to be fastidious or cantankerous; Don't have tantrums and don't frown. Have upbeat sentiments and See how well things turn out!

Do This: Choose glad emotions as opposed to getting steamed up.

Day 25
Be Quiet And Know That I Am God

(Be still, and know that I am God; I will be exalted among the heathen. I will be exalted in the earth. Psalm 46:10)

Shhhhhh. Be, still. God is surrounding you. Do you feel him? Would you be able to hear Him?

Do This: Think about God's miracles while you play the tranquil diversion (Quiet Game).

Day 26
"I Trust God. So I Am Not Afraid"

(In God I will praise his word, in God I have put my trust; I will not fear what flesh can do unto me. Psalm 56:4)

God will dependably deal with you. You never must be anxious again.

God will take care of You!

Do This: Tell God "thank you" for continually taking great care of you.

Day 27
Share With God's People

(Distributing to the necessity of saints; given to hospitality. Romans 12:13)

Be cheerful to share your toys with others. Check whether you can influence them to grin.

Do This: Let your companion play with your most loved toy today.

Day 28
"The Lord Is My Shepherd"

(The Lord is my shepherd; I shall not want. Psalm 23:1)

God takes great care of you. You are His little sheep. He is your solid defender.

Do This: Blow God an extraordinary huge kiss!

Day 29
Doing Right

(Give therefore thy servant an understanding heart to judge thy people, that I may discern between good and bad: for who is able to judge this thy so great a people? 1 Kings 3:9)

A few decisions are simple, similar to what you need to eat. Be that as it may, different decisions are harder: Should you tell your mother you inadvertently broke her most loved window box? We require God's assistance to use sound judgment. When we request God's assistance, he'll demonstrate to us what to do. Also, he'll give us the quality to on what's right side.

God can enable me to use sound judgment every day. At whatever point I ask him, he'll demonstrate to me the way.

Day 30
God's Wonderful World

(Remember his marvelous works that he hath done, his wonders, and the judgment of his mouth; 1 Chronicles 16:12)

The world is loaded with great things God made, similar to trees, blooms, grass, feathered creatures, and daylight. Is it accurate to say that it isn't amusing to squish your toes in the mud? Or, on the other hand sprinkle in a puddle? Or, then again get chilly snowflakes on your tongue? God made every one of these things so we would be cheerful. What a brilliant world! What a great God!

Much obliged to you, dear God, for the sky and the sun, For influencing a world where I to chuckle and have a ton of fun. I Thank so much dear God for everything!

Day 31
Follow The Leader

(And said, O Lord God of Israel, there is no God like thee in the heaven, nor in the earth; which keepeth covenant, and shewest mercy unto thy servants, that walk before thee with all their hearts: 2 Chronicles 6:14)

God keeps every one of his guarantees to us, regardless. What's more, he needs us to guarantee to tail him and do what he inquires. He needs us to be caring to others, tune in to our folks, and attempt our best to make the right decision. When we obey God, we demonstrate to him the amount we cherish him and that we are so happy to be his kids.

God, you are great. You do all that you say. Help me to love you and continuously comply.

Day 32
Who Loves You?

(And they sang together by course in praising and giving thanks unto the Lord; because he is good, for his mercy endureth for ever toward Israel. And all the people shouted with a great shout, when they praised the LORD, because the foundation of the house of the LORD was laid. Ezra 3:11)

In the event that you take a gander at a guide of the world, you can discover a nation called Israel. Yet, when the Bible uses the world Israel here, it implies the majority of God's kin. So when the Bible says God's affection for Israel goes on always, it implies that God adores you until the end of time! Doesn't that vibe incredible? I'm one of God's kin for the greater part of my days. He demonstrates to me his adoration in a wide range of ways.

Day 33
God Is Everywhere

(Thou, even thou, art LORD alone; thou hast made heaven, the heaven of heavens, with all their host, the earth, and all things that are therein, the seas, and all that is therein, and thou preservest them all; and the host of heaven worshipeth thee. Nehemiah 9:6)

We consider God when we go to church or read the Bible. In any case, God is all over. Despite the fact that we can't see him, we can see loads of things he made. So whenever you're outside, check out your neighborhood. Consider who influenced every one of the things you to see. The trees, the fowls, the mists all originate from God. Wherever you look, you can consider God and say thanks to him for making such an amazing world.

You made the sky and the trees and the fowls. Help me to thank you with awesome words.

Day 34
What Is God Like?

(And refused to obey, neither were mindful of thy wonders that thou didst among them; but hardened their necks, and in their rebellion appointed a captain to return to their bondage; but thou art a God ready to pardon, gracious and merciful, slow to anger, and of great kindness, and forsookest them not. Nehemiah 9:17)

Since we can't see God, it's difficult to comprehend what he resembles. Be that as it may, this Bible verse discloses to us he's all that we would ever need in a companion.

He generally pardons us when we accomplish something incorrectly, he's ease back to outrage with us, he comprehends what it resembles to be a child, and, a large portion of all, he cherishes us more than we can even envision. What an incredible companion!

Dear God, you are truly my best-of-all-companion. Furthermore, your love, your adoration for me will never end.

Day 35
Praise Him ……. with dancing

(Praise him with the timbrel and dance: praise him with stringed instruments and organs. Psalm 150:4)

King David moved for God energetically. Would you be able to move as well?

Do This: Jump and hit the dance floor with upbeat feet for God.

Day 36
"Hate What Is Evil"

(Let love be without dissimulation. Abhor that which is evil; cleave to that which is good. Romans 12:9)

Appreciate great things like: embraces, grins, and pleasant words. Avoid terrible things like: revolting talk, frowny countenances, and poor conduct.

Do This: Try to do three great things today and do them with your parents.

Day 37
"You Must Not Steal"

(Ye shall not steal, neither deal falsely, neither lie one to another. Leviticus 19:11)

Try not to take anything that doesn't have a place with you – notwithstanding when you outrageously need it. Ask before playing with a companion's things.

Do This: Put your companion's toys back when you are done playing.

Day 38
"I Will Tell All The Miracles You Have Done"

(I will praise thee, O LORD, with my whole heart; I will shew forth all thy marvellous works Psalm 9:1)

God likes for you to boast on Him as well. Tell everybody how great God is. Do This: Thank God for these things He has made.

Day 39
The Lord Is My Shepherd

(The LORD is my shepherd; I shall not want. Psalm 23:1)

God takes great care of you. You are His little sheep. He is your solid defender. Do This: Blow God an incredible enormous kiss.

Day 40
Be Kind And Loving To Each Other

(And be ye kind one to another, tenderhearted, forgiving one another, even as God for Christ's sake hath forgiven you. Ephesians 4:32)

Be caring and wanting to each other. Do pleasant things. Say decent things.

Do This: Do something decent for somebody today.

Day 41
A Good Man Takes Care Of His Animals

(A righteous man regardeth the life of his beast; but the tender mercies of the wicked are cruel. Proverbs 12:10)

Do you have a pet to play with? Do you have flying creatures in your trees? God likes it when we are decent to creatures.

Do This: Pat your pet delicately today

Day 42
A Greedy Person Brings Trouble To His Family

(He that is greedy of gain troubleth his own house; but he that hateth gifts shall live. Proverbs 15:27)

It's not pleasant to dependably take the greatest cut of cake. Appreciate the yummy piece you are given. Do This: Let another person have the greatest treat today.

Day 43
Count On God

(So the LORD blessed the latter end of Job more than his beginning: for he had fourteen thousand sheep, and six thousand camels, and a thousand yoke of oxen, and a thousand she asses. Job 42:12)

Did you realize that even the most grounded, most capable individual on the planet isn't as effective as God? Grown-ups are solid and keen, however some of the time regardless they have issues that appear to be too enormous for them. Be that as it may, every one of us can rely on God. So when you have an issue you can't settle, request that God offer assistance. Keep in mind that, he can do anything!

God, you are huge – you're the most grounded of all! I know you will help me at whatever point I call.

Day 44
Sleep Tight

(I will both lay me down in peace, and sleep; for thou, LORD, only makest me dwell in safety. Psalm 4:8)

God watches over all of you day long, regardless of where you go. However, did you know God even watches out for you while you rest? You don't need to be terrified of the dull or stress over having awful dreams. Simply recall that God is with you, ensuring you are protected throughout the night.

God watches over me all as the night progressed, Making beyond any doubt that I generally rest tight.

Day 45
Good Morning, God

(My voice shalt thou hear in the morning, O LORD, in the morning will I direct my prayer unto thee, and will look up. Psalm 5:3)

What's the main thing you do in the morning? Do you have breakfast or brush your teeth or cuddle with your folks? Regardless of how you begin your day, bear in mind to state great morning to God. Educate him regarding the day ahead. Reveal to him what really matters to you energized or anxious about or glad about.

Keep in mind, God's been with all of you night long, and he can hardly wait to get notification from you! In the morning, I will state Thank you, God, for this new day!

Day 46
Always Be Willing To Listen

(Wherefore, my beloved brethren, let every man be swift to hear, slow to speak, slow to wrath: James 1:19)

Continuously tune in, Listen. Give others a chance to talk as well. Tune in to what they need to state. Do This: Practice being a decent audience today. Listen!

Day 47
Strong Armor

(For in death there is no remembrance of thee: in the grave who shall give thee thanks? Psalm 5:12)

At the point when soldiers in Bible circumstances went to fight, they generally conveyed shields to ensure themselves. By what other means would they be able to remain safe from the stones and arrows their adversaries may toss at them? We won't not need to avoid rocks and arrows, but rather we as a whole have startling things to confront. It is ideal that we have God's affection to ensure us. It's a shield that will dependably protect us.

Since God's love is surrounding me, A shield of security will encompass me.

Day 48
Always Safe

(The LORD is my rock, and my fortress, and my deliverer, my God, my strength, in whom I will trust; my buckler, and the horn of my salvation, and my high tower. Psalms 18:2)

God dependably needs you to be protected. Your folks do as well. They do all that they can to take of you. Your mother dresses you warmly when it's chilly outside. Your father holds your hand when you cross a bustling road. In the event that your folks need to go some place, they request that somebody they put stock in remain with you. You can trust both your folks and God to protect you.

My Mom, my Dad, and God makes three. Together they take great care of me!

Day 49
Trust God

(Some trust in chariots, and some in horses: but we remember the name of the LORD our God. Psalm 20:7)

We as a whole like new garments, great nourishment, and bunches of toys. Furthermore, God needs us to appreciate every one of these things. Be that as it may, he doesn't need us to be glad just in the event that we have decent things. He needs us to be upbeat since he cherishes us, regardless of how much or how little we possess. What's more, when we believe him, we'll have all that we require, for eternity.

In spite of the fact that I like bunches of garments and toys – God's adoration and care are my greatest joys.

Day 50
Little Lambs

(The LORD is my shepherd; I shall not want. Psalm 23:1)

The Bible gabs about Jesus, God's Son, being our shepherd. It sounds interesting since we're not sheep. Yet, when the Bible says Jesus is our shepherd, it implies that he deals with us. A shepherd ensures his sheep have great nourishment to eat and a warm place to rest. He remains alert during the evening to keep wolves far from his rush. He guards them upbeat and both day and night. Also, much the same as a decent shepherd, Jesus tends to us, as well.

You are the shepherd – I am your sheep. You guard me wherever I am.

Day 51
Close Beside Me

(Yea, though I walk through the valley of the shadow of death, I will fear no evil: for thou art with me; they rod and thy staff they comfort me. Psalm 23:4)

At whatever point the leader of the United States goes some place, bunches of individuals run with him. Their employment is to ensure the president and ensure he's constantly sheltered. He's essential, and nobody needs him to get hurt. God is dependably with you, as well, wherever you go. He supposes you're important to the point that he needs to guard all of you day and throughout the night.

God, you ensure me wherever I go. You're generally close to me – you won't let me go. Thank You Lord, for protecting and remaining close to me.

Day 52
My Future

(Surely goodness and mercy shall follow me all the days of my life; and I will dwell in the house of the LORD for ever. Psalm 23:6)

What do you figure life will resemble later on? What will you grow up to be? Where will you live? No one truly comprehends what the future will resemble. In any case, we realize that whatever happens, God will be there, dealing with us and viewing over us.

As a result of you, God, my future looks splendid. Your affection and your goodness make everything right.

Day 53
Have No Fear!

(The LORD is my light and my salvation, whom shall I fear? The LORD is the strength of my life; of whom shall I be afraid? Psalm 27:1)

Life is brimming with new individuals, spots, and things. At first you may feel hesitant to meet another person, to go some place or somewhere you've never been, or have a go at something other than what's expected. In any case, recollect, you don't need to fear anything. You can be upbeat and appreciate all that life offers you!

With God next to me, I have nothing to fear. He guarantees me he will dependably be close.

Day 54
A Gift For God

(O love the LORD, all ye saints: for the LORD preserveth the faithful, and plentifully rewardeth the proud doer. Psalm 31:23)

God does as such numerous incredible things for us that it's pleasant when we can help out him, as well. In any case, what could God require? All things considered, God wants something from us – our adoration. We indicate God our adoration when we converse with him, when we believe him to help us, and when we obey him. Show God you cherish him today.

God, enable me to indicate you I adore you every single day, By all that I do and by all that I say.

Day 55
A Fresh Start

(For his anger endureth but a moment; in his favor is life; weeping may endure for a night, but joy cometh in the morning. Psalm 30:5)

Some days are hard. You may feel grouchy. Or, on the other hand perhaps you just can't remain out of inconvenience. Be that as it may, God allows you to begin once again every morning. Regardless of how terrible yesterday was, today is another day. Also, it's brimming with new opportunities to have some good times, to do decent things for other individuals, and to make new companions. Capitalize on this great new day!

Much obliged to you for giving me each shiny new day. Much obliged to you for taking my inconveniences away.

Day 56
All Gone

(Blessed is he whose transgression is forgiven, whose sin is covered. Psalm 32:1)

We as a whole commit errors, and afterward we more often than not feel tragic! We may offend someone, cause harm, or make our folks irate. Yet, God says he'll excuse our slip-ups when we reveal to him we're sad. Pardoning implies God takes away our missteps and acts like they never happened. What's more, that influences us to feel extremely cheerful.

God will excuse me when I commit errors. Saying "I'm sad is all that it takes.

Day 57
He's Always Watching

(I will instruct thee and teach in the way which thou shalt go; I will guide thee with mine eye. Psalm 32:8)

God is continually dealing with us. He gave us the Bible to enable us to comprehend what to do. He generally tunes in to our petitions. He places individuals in our lives, similar to guardians and educators and companions, to enable us to learn and develop and tail him. That is the means by which God watches out for each of us, consistently, until the end of time.

Through family and companions, God demonstrates to me the route – To do what he needs me to do each day.

Day 58
God Loves To Listen

(I sought the LORD, and he heard me, and delivered me from all my fears. Psalm 34:4)

Here and there it's difficult to envision an intense God setting aside opportunity to tune in to our little issues. Be that as it may, tuning in to you is one of God's most loved things to do. He adores you so much that he can hardly wait for you to call his name. Regardless of whether you're frightened or in a bad position, God guarantees that at whatever point you converse with him, he'll hear you and help you.

I'm never reluctant to have a go at something new. God tunes in to me, and he encourages me, as well!

Day 59
Big Trouble

(God is my refuge and strength, a very present help in trouble. Psalm 46:1)

Have you at any point had a truly awful day while everything turned out badly? The Bible says everybody will have issues. However, here's the colossal thing about inconvenience. When it comes, you're not the only one. God is there to help you. Also, he's more grounded and more capable than any of your inconveniences. He can enable you to traverse anything!

At the point when inconveniences comes, I don't need to stress. God's quality and power influence me to overcome in a rush.

Day 60
Always With Me

(For this God is our God for ever and ever; he will be our guide even unto death. Psalm 48:14)

Have you at any point been lost? It's a terrifying inclination would it say it isn't? When you get lost, you need somebody to point you the correct way and enable you to discover your direction. That is the thing that God improves the situation us. He demonstrates to us the correct bearing to go in life and sticks with us to ensure we never get lost. In the event that we hear him out and focus on his headings, we'll generally know exactly where to go.

With you as my guide there is one thing I know. You generally demonstrate to me which way I ought to go.

Day 61
God To The Rescue

(And call upon me in the day of trouble; I will deliver thee, and thou shalt glorify me. Psalm 50:15)

Do you have a puppy or feline in your family? Pets rely upon us to nourish them and deal with them. On the off chance that your pet is unnerved, you can enable it to feel safe. Also, God can enable you to feel safe as well! God salvages you from inconvenience, much the same as you would safeguard your pet in the event that it was in threat. You should simply put stock in God.

God, you guarantee to act the hero. When I'm in a bad position, I simply require to believe you.

Day 62
Anytime At All

(Evening, and mourning, and at noon, will I pray, and cry aloud: and he shall hear my voice. Psalm 55:17)

Do you know you can converse with God whenever you need? You can state a petition each prior night you go to bed. You can converse with him about your day when you initially get up in the morning. You can express gratitude toward him for your nourishment at lunch. Furthermore, you can converse with God whenever in the middle of – when you're playing with your toys, snickering with your companions, or at the recreation center with your father. Whenever is a decent time to converse with God!

God's prepared to listen when I need to talk. I can supplicate when I play, when I run, when I walk.

Day 63
God Is My Hero

(My Soul followeth hard after thee: thy right hand upholdeth me. Psalm 63:8)

Do you have a most loved superhuman? Superheroes on TV have stunning forces and can do nearly anything, But God is far and away superior to a hero. He secures you and deals with you in ways you can't see. He's the most effective, astounding superhuman you would ever need.

God's my saint, extraordinary and solid. Secure by him, I can't turn out badly.

Day 64
In God's Hands

(Which holdeth our soul in life, and suffereth not our feet to be moved. Psalm 66:9)

When you grasp some little animal, you must be extremely cautious. On the off chance that you press a little creature too firmly, it may get hurt. Yet, in the event that you don't hang on firmly enough, the animal may drop out of your hands and flee. You need to hold it without flaw. The Bible says God grasps our lives. He takes great care of us, holding us without flaw.

I'm in God's grasp, and he's holding me tight.
He deals with me each day and every night.

Day 65
Sunny Days

(For the Lord God is a sun and shield: the LORD will give grace and glory: no good thing will be withhold from them that walk uprightly. Psalm 84:11)

What might life resemble without the sun? All things considered, it would be extremely dull, for a certain something. Be that as it may, the sun accomplishes more than give us light. It keeps us warm and it enables things to develop. Everything on earth needs the sun to remain alive. The Bible says God is a sun. Without him, consistently would be dull and frosty and bleak.

In any case, with him, every day is brimming with light and warmth and satisfaction.

God gives us light, much the same as the sun. Without him, my life would not be as fun.

Day 66
My Favorite Things

(Yea, the LORD shall give that which is good; and our land shall yield her increase. Psalm 85:12)

Consider some of your most loved things (Your favorite things). Do you like creatures? blooms? bugs? apples? your grandmother? Where do you think your most favorite things originated from? The truth is out, God made them! Each good thing we have – from our loved ones to the yummy sustenance we eat – is a blessing from God. What's more, God will continue giving us great things for eternity. Everything great originates from God up above. The things that he gives us are the indications of his affection.

Day 67
First Aid

(In the day of my trouble I will call upon thee: for thou wilt answer me. Psalm 86:7)

Ouch! It harms when you tumble down and rub your knee! You raced to your mother, and she gives you a major embrace, cleans the rub, and puts a gauze on it. You quit crying and start to feel somewhat better, isn't that right? Despite the fact that scratches and wounds are unpleasant, realizing that God will dependably send you the assistance you require has a major effect.

I get out when I tumble down. I know an aide can be found.

Day 68
Tell Me A Story

(I will sing of the mercies of the LORD for ever; with my mouth will I make known thy faithfulness to all generations. Psalm 89:1)

You can take in loads of fascinating things from more seasoned human like your grandmother, your grandpa, or the pleasant neighbor down the piece. They can demonstrate to you generally accepted methods to angle, skip shakes, or make snow heavenly attendants. In any case, outstanding amongst other things more seasoned individuals can show you is the manner by which to confide in God. So whenever you're with individuals who have carried on quite a while, request that they disclose to you a tale about what God has improved the situation them. Their stories will enable you to recollect that God will dependably be with you, notwithstanding when you develop old. God will be with me as long as I live. Notwithstanding when I'm old, I'll have lots to give.

Day 69
Strong And Tall

(The righteous shall flourish like the palm tree; he shall grow like a cedar in Lebanon. Psalm 92:12)

Trees are a portion of the most established living things on the earth. A few trees are many years old! Trees are solid and can develop anyplace. They can stand hot sun and icy rain.

The Bible says we resemble trees. God made us ready to confront pretty much anything. With God's assistance, you can develop tall and solid as well, much the same as the trees.

I'll become solid and tall like a tree, Just the way God made me to be!

Day 70
Singing For Joy

(O COME, let us sing unto the LORD: let us make a joyful noise to the rock of our salvation. Psalm 95:1)

When you consider the amount God adores you, it's anything but difficult to get energized. You simply need to sing! You can think about your tune as a little supplication. You can disclose to God how extraordinary he is and that you are so happy to make them deal with you. So sing a tune and demonstrate the entire world the delight of cherishing God.

When I am cheerful, I will sing about the delight my God can bring!

Day 71
Forever Friends

(For the LORD is good; his mercy is everlasting; and his truth endureth to all generations. Psalm 100:5)

Do you know to what extent always or forever is? It's a ton longer than a week or a month or a year. Perpetually is such quite a while, to the point that it will never, ever end. Also, that is to what extent God's affection for you will keep going forever! That implies God will love you long after one week from now or one month from now or even one year from now is finished. God will love you longer than you can even envision.

God's adoration for me will never end. Always and Forever God will be my companion.

Day 72
Sky High

(For as the heaven is high above the earth, so great is his mercy toward them that fear him. Psalm 103:11)

It's far up to the sky, would it say it isn't? Would you be able to touch it when you hop? Would you be able to achieve the winged animal far up there? Would you be able to see where the sky closes? No! Furthermore, God's adoration is as colossal and astonishing as the sky. What's more, much the same as the sky, God's affection never, ever closes.

God's adoration for me is as large as the sky,
As wide and as clear and as enormous and as high.

Day 73
Long Gone

(As far as the east is from the west, so far hath he removed our transgressions from us. Psalm 103:12)

Sin is a little word with a major importance. Sins are the wrong things we do that hurt other individuals, such as lying or prodding or resisting. However, when we disclose to God we're sad, God takes those things away. Truth be told, he takes them so far away that even he doesn't see them any longer. So when we accomplish something we shouldn't, we can enlighten God regarding it, say we're sad, and realize that God will take the wrong we did far, far away.

When I foul up, what do I say? "I'm sad, God," and you take it away.

Day 74
Free As A Bird

(By them shall the fowls of the heaven have their habitation, which sing among the branches. Psalm 104:12)

Have you at any point seen that winged creatures (birds) dependably appear to be glad? They're continually singing. That is on account of God ensures winged creatures have all that they require. He gives them trees to live in, worms to eat, and water to drink. God gives us all that we require as well, isn't that right?

I can be cheerful, similar to a bird in a tree. Furthermore, much the same as a flying creature, God deals with me.

Day 75
Day By Day

(Thy people shall be willing in the day of thy power; in the beauties of holiness from the womb of the morning; thou hast the dew of thy youth. Psalm 110:3)

At the point when things throughout your life are hard, it's anything but difficult to get debilitated. Possibly your folks contend once in a while or somebody you cherish is debilitated. Or, then again perhaps your closest companion is moving without end. Be that as it may, God guarantees to enable you to overcome all your troublesome days. Request that he enable you to be solid today.

God will help me the distance. He gives me new strength step by step, and day by day.

Day 76
God's Special Book

(But our God is in the heavens: he hath done whatsoever he hath pleased. Psalm 115:3)

God lives in paradise or heaven. Be that as it may, he additionally is alive in his Word, the Bible. The Bible is loaded with important things God needs us to know. Furthermore, it's loaded with energizing stories about God and his reality. In the event that you need to become acquainted with God, the Bible is an awesome place to begin.

The Bible is God's unique book. When you require answer, look to the Bible.

Day 77
Never Too Busy

(I love the LORD, because he hathf heard my voice and my supplications. Psalm 116:1)

It's dreadful to converse with somebody who isn't generally tuning in. It's baffling when you need to recount somebody a story or pose an inquiry however everybody is excessively occupied with, making it impossible to tune in. In any case, God is never excessively caught up with, making it impossible to hear you out. When you have a remark him, simply say his name. He'll be there, prepared to hear you and help you.

God, you know I have parcels to state –
Thank you for tuning in to me today.

Day 78
Sweet Dreams

(The LORD is on my side; I will not fear: what can man do unto me?Psalm 118:6)

At the point when it's the ideal opportunity for bed, you may not generally like being separated from everyone else in your dim room. In any case, Jesus is with you, even oblivious, even amidst the night. He ensures you notwithstanding when you're sleeping. So you don't need to fear the dull. Simply recall Jesus is viewing over you. He'll enable you to rest soundly – and you'll have great dreams.

I am protected when my day closes,
Dreaming dreams that Jesus sends.

Day 79
Words To Go

(Thy word have I hid in mine heart, that I might not sin against thee. Psalm 119:11)

The Bible is brimming with guarantees from God. Heaps of them are found in the book of Psalms. You've been perusing some of them every day in this book. You can take in the ones you like best by heart. At that point God's words will be with all of you the time!

God's Word is with me wherever I go. The Bible is brimming with great things to know.

Day 80
Lasting Love

(Thy faithfulness is unto all generations: thou hast established the earth, and it abideth. Psalm 119:90)

The earth has been around quite a while. What's more, since the absolute starting point, God has adored the general population on earth. He cherished and tended to your folks when they were little quite recently like you. He viewed over your grandparents and your great – grandparents, as well! The earth was worked to keep going quite a while, and God's loyalty and love will last much more!

The affection for God will last and last, Even when this day has passed.

Day 81
Shine The Light

(Thy word is a lamp unto my feet, and a light unto my path. Psalm 119:105)

Going out for a stroll outside during the very late evening (night) can be loads of fun. In any case, you require a spotlight to enable you to see where you're going so you won't trip or get lost. The Bible resembles an electric lamp. It causes us see where we ought to go and demonstrates to us the correct way to take.

God's Word will constantly light my direction. It instructs me and tells me what to say.

Day 82
The Greatest Helper

(I will lift up mine eyes unto the hills, from whence cometh my help. Psalm 121:1)

God gives you loads of individuals to love you and help you. Your folks can enable you to make sense of what to do when you're befuddled. The specialist can improve you feel when you're debilitated. Your closest companion can brighten you up when you're pitiful. God gave you guardians to love you and specialists to keep you solid and companions to influence you to chuckle. God gives all of you the assistance you require!

When I require enable, who to would i be able to call? I approach God, Creator of all.

Day 83
Wide Awake

(He will not suffer thy foot to be moved; he that keepeth thee will not slumber. Behold, he that keepeth Israel shall neither slumber nor sleep. Psalm 121:3-4)

Your mother and father do their absolute best to deal with you. Be that as it may, now and again you may even now get hurt. On the off chance that you tumble down, they need to be there to help you. God loves to help you, as well. Much the same as your folks, God needs you to be protected. Be that as it may, dissimilar to your folks, who can't be wakeful constantly, God never dozes. He never takes his eyes off of you.

God watches me every night and day. When I'm sleeping, and when I am at play.

Day 84
Watching Over You

(The LORD is thy keeper; the LORD is thy shade upon thy right hand. The sun shall not smite thee by day, nor the moon by night. Psalm 121:5-6)

God is continually viewing over you. He is never excessively occupied. God, the Creator of the entire world, watches over you himself, 24 hours every day. You never must be anxious or think about whether God is truly around. Regardless of whether you're conscious or snoozing, God is in that spot with you.

God's not very occupied to watch over me. There's nothing I do that he can't see.

Day 85
Safe In The Storm

(The LORD shall preserve thy going out and thy coming in from this time forth, and even for evermore. Psalm 121:7)

Have you at any point been out in the rain without an umbrella? You get wet and frosty and awkward. Umbrellas are incredible for keeping you dry. All things considered, God is similar to an umbrella. He protects you and gives you a sheltered place to avoid the things that may hurt you. Yet, not at all like an umbrella, God is dependably with you. You don't need to chase for him in your storeroom!

At the point when life is a struggle, God's close by. He is dependably a sheltered place to stow away.

Day 86
The Best Present

(Lo, children are an heritage of the LORD and the fruit of the womb is his reward. Psalm 127:3)

What's the best present you've at any point been given? An amusement? A trek to the zoo for your birthday? It's dependably enjoyable to get blessings, particularly ones you truly like. Did you know God gave your folks an exceptional blessing? You!!! The day you turned out to be a piece of your family is a day your folks will always remember. Get some information about the best present they at any point got. They'll disclose to you it's you!

God gave my folks a blessing, you see. That brilliant, great blessing is me!

Day 87
Thank You!

(O Give thanks unto the LORD; for he is good: for his mercy endureth for ever. Psalm 136:1)

At the point when a companion accomplishes something pleasant for you, it makes you cheerful. You grin and say, "Thank you!" God does heaps of pleasant things for you as well. Also, he adores it when you say thank you to him. Whenever you see one of the magnificent things God has given you, similar to a comfortable bed or a bright morning, make certain to state thank you God!

I have so much I can express gratitude toward God for – My home, my family, my companions, and more.

Day 88
Food For You

(Who giveth food to all flesh; for his mercy endureth for ever. Psalm 136:25)

At the point when God made us, he knew we'd have to eat, so he gave us sustenance. An extraordinary nourishment, but rather ridiculously great sustenance. The jam in your sandwich began as a grape God developed. The drain in your container originated from a dairy animals God made. Chocolate, frozen yogurt, and even pizza are altogether produced using God's great fixings. God beyond any doubt is a great culinary specialist!

God has given me nourishment to eat – Fruits and veggies and my most loved treats.

Day 89
Questions And Answers

(In the day when I cried thou answeredst me, and strengthened me with strength in my soul. Psalm 138:3)

Did you ever petition God for a comment and it didn't? When you request a child sibling and get a sister rather or ask that your grandpa will show signs of improvement and he doesn't, you may figure God isn't tuning in. Be that as it may, God truly answers every one of our petitions. He replies by helping us figure out how to love the infant he sent us, or by ameliorating us when somebody we adore is wiped out. God may not generally give us the appropriate response we need, but rather he'll generally give us the appropriate response we require.

God has answers for the greater part of my petitions. His answer's a guarantee to dependably be there.

Day 90
The Buddy System

(Though I walk in the midst of trouble, thou wilt revive me: thou shalt stretch forth thine hand against the wrath of mine enemies, and thy right hand shall save me. Psalm 138:7)

Have you at any point been accomplishing something and after that required somebody to help you? At the point when help arrived, you presumably began to feel better immediately. Frequently all we truly require is someone else to enable us to out. With a companion to help us, our concern doesn't appear to be so huge any longer. Regardless of what happens, recall forget God guarantees to send you the assistance you require. I'm never alone, so I don't have to fear. Regardless of what happens, help is always close.

Day 91
Big Plans

(The LORD will perfect that which concerneth me: thy mercy, O LORD, endureth for ever; forsake not the works of thine own hands. Psalm 138:8)

It's enjoyable to dream about what's to come. You can envision being a ballet dancer or a motion picture star or a football player. You don't comprehend what our life will resemble when you grow up, yet God does. He's given you unique endowments and abilities to help improve the world a place. Together you and God will have an awesome splendid future.

Who knows what the future will be? Yet, God has bunches of plans for me.

Day 92
A Special Creation

(O LORD, thou hast searched me, and known me. Thou hast beset me behind and before, and laid thine hand upon me. Psalm 139:1,5)

When you paint a photo, you pick the colors you need and put them where you figure they ought to go. When you make a snowman, you choose where his nose ought to be. When you influence something, you to know every little thing about it. At the point when God made you, he chose all parts and set up them together. So he knows and cherishes every little thing about you. You are his unique creation.

God knows me well, all around. He realizes what truly matters to me.

Day 93
Here, There, And Everywhere

(If I take the wings of the morning, and dwell in the uttermost parts of the sea; Even there shall thy hand lead me, and thy right hand shall hold me. Psalm 139:9-10)

The world is brimming with fascinating spots to go. Going on a plane interestingly is extremely energizing. So is riding on a prepare or cruising on a lake! Be that as it may, regardless of where you go – in the midst of a furlough, to your grandparents' home, to another nation – God is there with you. In every one of your enterprises, God is close by.

Wherever I go, whatever I do, I generally realize that God's there, as well.

Day 94
Made With Love

(For thou hast possessed my reins: thou hast covered me in my mother's womb. Psalm 139:13)

You know God cherishes you. Be that as it may, did you know he cherished you even before you were conceived? God's the person who made you and set up you together inside your mother. God's the person who chose what shading your eyes ought to be and to what extent your nose ought to be. God made you painstakingly so you'd be perfect. Furthermore, you are!

Dear God, you gave me my hands and my hair. You made me with adoration. You made me with mind.

Day 95
Wonderful You

(I will praise thee; for I am fearfully and wonderfully made; marvelous are thy works, and that my soul knoweth right well. Psalm 139:14)

Do you ever think your feet are too enormous or your eyes are excessively dark colored? Truly, God needed each of us to be one of a kind. He made you precisely the way he however you ought to be. At the point when God takes a gander at you, he doesn't see huge feet or eyes excessively dark colored. He sees somebody he adores, somebody he supposes is brilliant!

God made me unique, I know it's valid. I am astonishing and awesome, as well!

Day 96
First Things First

(Thy kingdom is an everlasting kingdom, and thy domain endureth throughout all generations. Psalm 145:13)

The Bible is loaded with verses that help us to remember God's guarantees and his adoration for us. Possibly you've been asking why the Bible continues saying a similar thing again and again. This is on the grounds that the most vital lesson the Bible shows us is that God adores us more than we can envision. Furthermore, that merits rehashing!

The Bible is brimming with God's words from above. The best expression of all is his magnificent love.

Day 97
Need A Lift

(The LORD upholdeth all that fall, and raised up all those that be bowed down. Psalm 145:14)

Each family experiences intense circumstances. Now and then somebody we adore bites the dust, or there isn't much cash for the sake of entertainment things, or mothers and fathers experience considerable difficulties getting along. It's amid those circumstances that God guarantees to lift us up and prop us up. That doesn't mean the intense circumstances will leave in a moment, however it implies you don't need to experience only them.

God causes me through great circumstances and awful. He's even there when I feel pitiful.

Day 98
Keep Talking

(The LORD is nigh unto all them that call upon him, to all that call upon him in truth. Psalm 145:18)

Despite the fact that God is intense, he's not startling to converse with. You may figure just essential individuals can converse with God, or that you need to utilize uncommon words or be in an extraordinary place to supplicate. However, God tunes in to everybody, regardless of their identity or what words they utilize or where they may be. So when you require God, simply begin talking!

Wherever I am, whatever I say, God's prepared to hear me out when I pray.

Day 99
God Promised!

(Which made heaven, and earth, the sea, and all that therein is: which keepeth truth for ever. Psalm 146:6)

God made heaps of guarantees in the Bible. He guaranteed Noah that he'd never send another surge and afterward gave Noah a rainbow to enable him to recall. He guaranteed Abraham and Sarah that they'd have an infant, despite the fact that they were more established than your grandparents. He guaranteed the Israelites they would dependably have enough to eat, notwithstanding when they were living in the abandon. What's more, God kept each and every one of those guarantees. At the point when God says he'll accomplish something he would not joke about this.

At the point when God makes a guarantee, he'll generally come through.

He keeps each guarantee to me and to you.

Day 100
Nice To Hear!

(Let every thing that hath breath praise the LORD. Praise ye the LORD. Psalm 150:6)

There's nothing superior to having somebody say decent things in regards to you. You feel great when your mother discloses to you you're keen. Or, on the other hand when your instructor says you made an incredible showing with regards to taking in your numbers. Or, on the other hand when a companion reveals to you you're amusing. God love to hear decent things as well. So reveal to him how magnificent he is. Say the amount you adore him and how appreciative you are for all he's improved the situation you! Saying decent things is so natural to do.

Day 101
A Parent's Job

(My son, hear the instruction of thy father, and forsake not the law of thy mother: Proverbs 1:8)

Do you know why your mother and father dependably guide you and how to do it? As a matter of fact, it's their employment! God gave you guardians to show you how to deal with yourself. He needs you to be sound and glad as you grow up. That is the reason it's imperative to focus on what your folks say and do what they inquire.

God gave me guardians to enable me to develop, To love me and show me the things I should know.

Day 102
Everywhere I Look

(Turn you at my reproof: behold, I will pour out my spirit unto you. I will make known my words unto you. Proverbs 1:23)

Did you know God is dependably around, despite the fact that you can't see him? Wherever you look, you can see indications of God's essence. The trees, the blossoms, the flying creatures, and the butterflies are on the whole indications of God's adoration and the guarantees he's made. Each time you see something God made, recollect that he is with you.

Wherever I look, I can't resist the urge to see God's work in the blossoms, flowers and trees.

Day 103
Good Gifts

(Let not mercy and truth forsake thee: bind them about thy neck; write them upon the table of thine heart. Proverbs 3:3)

What are two of the best endowments you can give a companion? Dedication and benevolence. Faithfulness implies staying up for your companion, regardless of the possibility that different sorts ridicule her or him. It's being companions with somebody regardless. generosity is considering your companion's sentiments. It's doing decent things for him or her, such as giving them a chance to play with your most loved toy for an entirety. When you're faithful and kind, you'll never come up short on companions!

Help me, God, to be a decent companion – One who is thoughtful and kind and there until the end.

Day 104
Learning New Things

(Trust in the LORD with all thine heart; and lean not unto thine own understanding. Proverbs 3:5)

Have you at any point needed to accomplish something however experienced considerable difficulties making sense of it! Perhaps it was figuring out how to tie your shoes. You attempted and attempted, however regardless you required some assistance. It's difficult to do things without anyone else. That is the reason God needs us to request enable when we to require it. God gave us minds that can learn new things. God encourages me learn things that are new, From perusing a book to tying my shoe.

Day 105
Wise And Smart

(Happy is the man that findeth wisdom, and the man that getteth understanding. For the merchandise of silver, and the gain thereof than fine gold. Proverbs 3:13-14)

A standout amongst other parts of growing up is finding how to do new things. Figuring out how to dress yourself or compose your name or read a book is energizing. As you learn, you're getting something the Bible calls shrewdness. Intelligence implies using sound judgment and following God. So continue learning!

On the off chance that you need to be savvy and keen, Just take after God with your entire being.

Day 106
Bedtime Promises

(When thou liest down, thou shalt not be afraid; yea, thou shalt lie down, and thy sleep shall be sweet. Proverbs 3:24)

Before you know it, it's a great opportunity to prepare for bed! Now and again it's difficult to settle down and nod off. You wish you could play for a little time longer. You'd like somebody to peruse you only one more story. Be that as it may, your body needs an entire night's rest so you can have a great time each day. So cuddle under your spreads and close your eyes.

Furthermore, recollect that God guarantees to give you sweet dreams!

God, you are with me when I go to bed, putting sweet dreams within my head.

Day 107
Step By Step

(For the LORD shall be thy confidence, and shall keep thy foot from being taken. Proverbs 3:26)

What might manage without your feet? You won't consider them much, but rather you utilize them a ton! Your feet enable you amusing to quick and bounce high. With your feet you can kick a ball, pedal a bike, stroll here and there huge slopes, or ride a skateboard. When you have a go at something new, express gratitude toward God for your two in number feet. Also, recall, he's with you at all times.

God is with you, there's no compelling reason to fear. With each progression you take, God will be close.

Day 108
God Is Awesome

(The fear of the LORD is the beginning of wisdom: and the knowledge of the holy is understanding. Proverbs 9:10)

Why might the Bible say you should "fear" God? All things considered, God is your absolute best companion. What's more, you shouldn't be terrified of a companion, isn't that so? In any case, God is more than a companion. He's the considerable and effective Creator of the entire universe! To "fear" God truly implies you regard him and recall how magnificent he is.

God is amazing and capable, as well. However he's a companion to both me and you!

Day 109
Real Love

(Hatred stirreth up strifes; but love covereth all sins. Proverbs 10:12)

Have you at any point been frantic (Mad) at your mother or father? You're not alone! All children get frantic at their folks. In any case, when you adore somebody, it's difficult to remain frantic at them for long. Adoring others implies you excuse them when they commit errors. It implies you're caring to them, regardless of the possibility that they're not generally kind to you. A large portion of all, cherishing others implies you think about them the way God thinks about you.

When I get irate at those I cherish, I can at present love them with assistance from above.

Day 110
Helping Hands

(The liberal soul shall be made fat; and he that watereth shall be watered also himself. Proverbs 11:25)

Would you be able to think about an approach to enable somebody you to love? What about helping your younger sibling or younger sibling get dressed? Or, on the other hand doing the dishes without being inquired? You can bolster the pooch or the fish or exhaust the trash can or rake clears out. All these are awesome approaches to indicate love to others. How might you help somebody today?

When I help other people and do what I should, it reveals to them I adore them and influences me to rest easy.

Day 111
Deep Roots

(A man shall not be established by wickedness; but the root of the righteous shall not be moved. Proverbs 12:3)

Have you at any point seen a tree that is tumbled down after a major tempest? Solid breezes and substantial rain can pull even the greatest tree up by its underlying foundations. However, trees that have establishes somewhere down in the ground are significantly more prone to remain standing, regardless of how solid the tempest. God needs us to plant our "foundations" in him. The more we think about him and the more we believe him, the more profound our underlying foundations will go. What's more, those roots will enable us to stand up in great circumstances and in terrible circumstances.

Much the same as a tree, my underlying foundations are solid. I'll confide in God my entire long lasting.

Day 112
You Promised

(Lying lips are abomination to the LORD: but they that deal truly are his delight. Proverbs 12:22)

It's anything but difficult to make a promise, would it say it isn't? Perhaps you promised to make your bed or bolster the canine. But on the other hand it's anything but difficult to get occupied with accomplishing something different and neglect to do what you promised. Some of the time it's difficult to keep a promise! In any case, doing what you say you'll do is an indication that you're growing up. So stay faithful to your promise! You can rely on me to do what I say!

Day 113
Trues Riches

(There is that maketh himself rich, yet hath nothing; there is that maketh himself poor, yet hath great riches. Proverbs 13:7)

To a few people, cash is vital. Yet, cash can't purchase the things that truly make you cheerful, similar to companions or fun or love. Obviously it's decent to have cash. At that point you can purchase heaps of toys. However, having companions to giggle with and a family that affections you is stunningly better than toys. On the off chance that you have God in your heart and individuals who adore you, you're the wealthiest child around the local area!

With family and companions and days that are bright, I can be rich with no cash!

Day 114
A Gentle Answer

(A Soft answer turneth away wrath: but grievous words stir up anger. Proverbs 15:1)

When somebody gets furious with you, it's anything but difficult to get irate ideal back. Before you know it, everybody is shouting or crying. However, issues are explained significantly more rapidly in the event that you remain quiet. On the off chance that you talk mercifully to others notwithstanding when you're annoyed with them (or they're angry with you), you'll be giving a "delicate answer." And God will be satisfied with you! Since I am thoughtful, I won't yell. I'll attempt to remain quiet and work things out.

Day 115
Feel Better Fast!

(A Wholesome tongue is a tree of life: but perverseness therein is a breach in the spirit. Proverbs 15:4)

How would you feel when you need to play baseball and it begins to rain? Or, on the other hand when you need a sausage for lunch and there are just ground sirloin sandwiches? Things don't generally go the way you need them to. However, crying and griping doesn't offer assistance. It aggravates you feel even. So whenever things don't go your path, consider the great parts of your day. It won't take ache for you to rest easy!

Notwithstanding when things don't go my direction, I can discover something great to state.

Day 116
A Big Smile

(A merry heart maketh a cheerful countenance; but by sorrow of the heart the spirit is broken. Proverbs 15:13)

What do you do when you're cheerful? do you chuckle? sing? run? bounce? container? snicker? Everybody demonstrate bliss in an unexpected way. In any case, there's one thing we as a whole do. We as a whole grin. At the point when your heart feels glad, a grin can't resist climbing onto your face and staying nearby for some time. So sing and laugh and hop and grin. You have such a great amount to be glad about!

When I am cheerful, I simply need to grin. And after that my grin will remain for some time!

Day 117
Little Things

(Commit thy works unto the LORD, and thy thoughts shall be established. Proverbs 16:3)

God thinks about all that you do. He's glad when you converse with him and read about him in the Bible. He's satisfied when you draw a photo, play with your brother or sister, or get your garments. God is keen on all that you do, from the seemingly insignificant details to the huge ones as well! Make sure to reveal to him every one of your plans!

God, I reveal to all of you my plans. Of all shapes and sizes, you get it!

Day 118
Trust And Obey

(He that handleth a matter wisely shall find good: and whoso trusteth in the LORD, happy is he. Proverbs 16:20)

The Bible says the best approach to be truly glad is to trust God and obey him. When you trust and comply, your heart is brimming with adoration. Your psyche is brimming with great musings. You need to do kind and supportive things for the general population around you. You appreciate each snapshot of consistently. Since you put stock in God to deal with you, you are glad and favored!

God deals with me consistently. I am glad and favored when I comply!

Day 119
Kind Words

(Pleasant words are as an honeycomb, sweet to the soul, and health to the bones. Proverbs 16:24)

Consider how great it feels when somebody discloses to you how superb you are. Wouldn't it be decent to make another person feel that great? Have a go at educating a companion what you like regarding him or her. Or, then again let one know of your folks how happy you are that God made you a family. Say thank you to your educator; tell grandma you cherish her, make proper acquaintance with the new kid or new young lady nearby. A little thoughtfulness can fill somebody's heart with joy.

Expressions of consideration dependably can rest easy, So share them with your neighborhood!

Day 120
A Real Friend

(A friend loveth at all times, and a brother is born for adversity. Proverbs 17:17)

It's amusing to play with your companions when everybody is getting along. Be that as it may, imagine a scenario in which somebody says something intend to another person. You could participate and be mean as well. Be that as it may, a genuine companion goes to bat for others, notwithstanding when they are being prodded. It's not generally simple to be a dedicated companion. Be that as it may, God needs us to be benevolent and help each other. He'll give you the mettle to be a genuine companion. At the point when companions of mine are being prodded, I support them and God is satisfied.

Day 121
Be A Blessing

(The just man walketh in his integrity; his children are blessed after him. Proverbs 20:7)

Individuals come in all shapes, sizes, and hues. God gave everybody diverse abilities and gifts, as well. That is the reason our reality is such an intriguing spot. Be that as it may, regardless of what you look like or what sort of gifts you have, God needs you to be great and carry on with a genuine life. In the event that you do, you will dependably be a gift to others.

A few people are short, a few people are tall, But the individuals who are good eclipse them all.

Day 122
Do Your Best

(He that followeth after righteousness and mercy findeth life, righteousness, and honour. Proverbs 21:21)

God realizes that nobody is great. We as a whole commit errors. In any case, we can attempt to do our absolute best each day. We can request that God help us to be great, adoring, and kind. So you don't need to stress over being great. God is glad when you simply put forth a valiant effort.

No one's ideal, and that is alright! God encourages me do my best every day.

Day 123
God Loves Me

(Train up a child in the way he should go; and when he is old, he will not depart from it. Proverbs 22:6)

When you were a child, you couldn't do quite a bit of anything with the exception of eat and rest and look adorable. What's more, now take a gander at you! You can walk, talk, tell jokes, and sing melodies. Your folks helped you take in every one of these things. They need to show you as much as they would so be able to you will experience the correct way. Yet, the most vital thing you can gain from your folks is that God cherishes you in particular!

Of the considerable number of things I learn as I develop, God's adoration for me is the best thing to know!

Day 124
Word Power

(A word fitly spoken is like apples of gold in pictures of silver. Proverbs 25:11)

Did you know you have the ability to change somebody's entire day? That power is inside your mouth! The words you say can change the way someone else feels. In the event that somebody is dismal, a kind word from you can enable her or him to rest easy. In the event that somebody is stressed, quiet words can enable him to unwind. Consider the words you say. They can have a major effect to another person!

Enable me to recollect that my words are solid. They have the ability to settle what isn't right.

Day 125
Friends Are Fun

(Thine own friend, and thy father's friend, forsake not; neither go into thy brother's house in the day of thy calamity: for better is a neighbor that is near than a brother far off. Proverbs 27:10)

Companions are unique endowments from God. You can never have an excessive number of companions! Companions are enjoyable to be with, regardless of whether you are going some place exceptional or simply playing in your patio. They can transform a drilling day into a fun enterprise. Genuine companions love each other regardless. Say thanks to God for good companions!

Companions are surely one of God's blessings. They cherish you and embrace you and give you a lift. Never abandon a friend!

Day 126
Perfect Timing

(To every thing there is a season, and a time to every purpose under the heaven: Ecclesiastes 3:1)

It is difficult to be tolerant when you need a remark. Sitting tight for your birthday to come or for summer to begin can be so difficult! However, God has a period for everything. He influenced the seasons to sufficiently long for blooms and trees to develop. He influenced the days to sufficiently long for both work and play. When you get restless, recollect that everything happens precisely when God needs it to. His circumstances is the ideal time. God's responsible for the days and the seasons, He designs everything for the best of reasons.

Day 127
Friends For You

(For if they fall, the one will lift up his fellow; but woe to him that is alone when he falleth; for he hath not another to help him up. Ecclesiastes 4:10)

Aren't you happy you have companions? Companions are continually eager to help you. A companion can improve you feel when you're tragic. A companion can enable you up when you to tumble down and get hurt. God demonstrates you he cherishes you by giving you great companions. Furthermore, when you nurture your companions, you're demonstrating to them God's adoration as well.

I am happy I have companions to help when I'm tragic. My companions will be with me through great circumstances and awful.

Day 128
Helping Out

(Every man also to whom God hath given riches and wealth, and hath given him power to eat thereof, and to take his portion, and to rejoice in his labour; this is the gift of God. Ecclesiastes 5:19)

What errands do you need to do? Set the table? Nourish the pooch? Clean your room? Tasks aren't generally fun, however they are an essential piece of being a family. At the point when everybody assists with the work, there's more opportunity for entertainment only. So do your errands with a grin. You're helping your family and making your home an extraordinary place to live!

Working is hard and is not generally fun, But rather a grin will help you to take care of business.

Day 129
Wise Words

(The words of a wise man's mouth are gracious; but the lips of a fool will swallow up himself. Ecclesiastes 10:12)

Grown-ups give kids a wide range of guidelines; "Stand up straight." "Don't put your elbows on the table." "Eat your vegetables." "Brush your teeth." It's great to take after these directions since they show us acceptable behavior. The Bible gives us heaps of guidelines as well, similar to "Love God" and "Love others." The Bible says we will be cheerful in the event that we tune in to these directions and do what they say.

Astute words make me glad and great. I hear them out and do what I should.

Day 130
Give With A Smile!

(Cast thy bread upon the waters; for thou shalt find it after many days. Ecclesiastes 11:1)

In some cases you might not have any desire to share your toys. All things considered, that implies letting another person have something you need. Be that as it may, when you share, you typically recover your toys. Offering a comment individual for the long haul can be significantly harder than sharing. Be that as it may, when you give somebody a blessing, attempt to give it with a grin. When you do, they'll give a grin appropriate back to you. What's more, a grin is an awesome blessing! Giving a blessing influences me to grin, I feel useful for a long time!

Day 131
Happy Thoughts

(Truly the light is sweet, and a pleasant thing it is for the eyes to behold the sun. Rejoice, O young man, in thy youth, and let thy heart cheer thee in the days of thy youth, and walk in the ways of thine heart, and in the sight of thine eyes; but know thou, that for all these things God will bring thee into judgment. Ecclesiastes 11:7,9)

You can simply discover a comment about. Yet, being alive is brilliant! You get the opportunity to bounce in puddles and grapple with your father and eat chocolate chip treats and appreciate the daylight. Life is a ton of fun! Rather than griping about the things that don't appear to be correct, why not express gratitude toward God? He's the person who gave you this brilliant life loaded with awesome individuals and things.

Much obliged to you, God, for this brilliant day. I need to appreciate it inside and out!

Day 132
Your Very Own Voice

(Cry out and shout, thou inhabitant of Zion; for great is the Holy One of Israel in the midst of thee. Isaiah 12:6)

God gave you your own one of a kind voice. Furthermore, it doesn't seem like anybody else's! You utilize your voice for talking. The more words you take in, the more you can talk! In any case, you can likewise utilize your voice for singing. When you are cheerful, singing a melody is a decent approach to demonstrate it. God loves to hear your cheerful voice! When I feel glad I'll sing a melody. In case you're glad as well, you can chime in!

Day 133
Always Learning

(This also cometh forth from the LORD of hosts, which is wonderful in counsel, and excellent in working. Isaiah 28:29)

It's astounding the amount you can learn in only one day. Just today you may have figured out how to swim or compose your name or catch your shirt. What's more, think about every one of the things God has indicated you today! He's demonstrated to you the amount he cherishes you by giving you a family. He's demonstrated to you how well he deals with you by helping your folks get you garments and sustenance. He's even demonstrated to you the amount he needs you to have a fabulous time by giving you such huge numbers of exercises to appreciate. Envision what he has in store for you tomorrow!

I have loads of developing to do, Learning new things my entire life through.

Day 134
Quiet Time

(For thus saith the Lord God, the Holy One of Israel; In returning and rest shall ye be saved' om quietness and in confidence shall be your strength: and ye would not. Isaiah 30:15)

Would you be able to hear somebody whisper in a room loaded with clamor? No! You must be still and calm to hear a whisper. As intense as God may be, now and then he gets a kick out of the chance to address us in a tranquil whisper. That implies we have to take a little time each day to be still and tune in to God. When we do, we'll hear his words whispered in our heart. When I am peaceful and still as can be, God's voice whispers delicately to me!

Day 135
Talking With God

(And therefore will the LORD wait, that he may be gracious unto you, and therefore will he be exalted, that he may have mercy upon you: for the Lord is a God of judgment; blessed are all they that wait for him. Isaiah 30:18)

Life can get truly bustling now and then. You have companions to converse with, diversions to play, and books to peruse. It can be difficult to press in all that you need to do in a day. However, God is continually sitting tight for you to come and converse with him. Regardless of how bustling you are, God's constantly prepared to tune in and prepared to offer assistance. So spare a couple of minutes every day to converse with God.

There are books to peruse and diversions to play, But regardless I'll converse with God today!

Day 136
God The King

(For the LORD is our judge, the LORD is our lawgiver, the LORD is our King; he will save us. Isaiah 33:22)

When you think about a lord, what do you consider? Somebody who's capable? Somebody you simply need to comply? Somebody who's responsible for everything and everybody? Indeed, that is God! He's every one of those things and then some. He's cherishing and kind. He's prepared to pardon our missteps. He ensures we have all that we should be solid and upbeat. He's superior to any ruler here on earth. What's more, he's the main King will's identity around until the end of time!

Much thanks to you, God, for being my ruler. I adore you more than anything.

Day 137
Forever And Ever

(The grass withereth, the flower fadeth but the word of our God shall stand for ever. Isaiah 40:8)

There are bunches of things on the planet, similar to mountains and seas, that have been around since God made them a long time back. In any case, even the mountains and seas will be gone one day. The main thing that will keep going forever is God's affection for us. That is the reason we put our trust in God. He will be here notwithstanding while everything else is gone.

God's affection is everlastingly, it will never kick the bucket. He will last longer than earth, ocean, or sky.

Day 138
Our Shepherd

(He shall feed his flock like a shepherd; he shall gather the lambs with his arm, and carry them in his bosom, and shall gently lead those that are with young. Isaiah 40:11)

God is extraordinary and capable, however he is exceptionally delicate, as well. He watches over us the way a decent shepherd tends to his sheep. on the off chance that a little sheep gets hurt, the shepherd conveys the sheep until the point that it can rest easy. What's more, when the sheep have babies, the shepherd encourages them locate a sheltered place to eat and rest. The shepherd adores his sheep and does all that he can to tend to them. God is our shepherd, and we are his little sheep.

God is my shepherd and I am his sheep. He protects me wherever I am!

Day 139
Full Of Power

(He giveth power to the faint; and to them that have no might he increaseth strength. Isaiah 40:29)

Our bodies are stunning! Eating nourishment that is beneficial for us, getting heaps of activity, and getting enough rest are all ways we can enable our bodies to remain solid and sound. Yet, notwithstanding when we take better than average care of ourselves, we can in any case get frail and tired. Buckling down can influence us to get a handle on worn at times! God guarantees to give additional quality for those circumstances. Simply ask him!

When I am worn out and feeling powerless, God's quality gives me the assistance I look for!

Day 140
Fly Like An Eagle

(But they that wait upon the LORD shall renew their strength, they shall mount up with wings as eagles; they shall run, and not be weary; and they shall walk, and not faint. Isaiah 40:31)

Have you at any point seen a Eagle? Eagles can fly spots different flying creatures can't. They want to fly high in the sky and take off on the breeze. The Bible discloses to us that we can be as solid as a eagle with God's assistance. We can go places we didn't know we could go and do things we didn't know we could do. When you're having a hard day, request that God lift you up and move you solid like a eagle. When I'm disheartened and don't know why, God gives me quality and causes me to fly.

Day 141
A Helping Hand

(Fear thou not; for I am with thee; be not dismayed' for I am thy God. I will strengthen thee; yea, I will help thee; yea, I will uphold thee with the right hand of my righteousness. Isaiah 41:10)

It's not generally simple being a youngster. Somebody's continually revealing to you you're excessively youthful or too small, making it impossible to do the things you need to do. Be that as it may, God causes you develop more grounded each day. Not very far in the past, you required help getting dressed, having lunch, and tallying to ten. Presently you might have the capacity to do those things without anyone else's input! Whenever somebody discloses to you you're too little to accomplish something, recall that God is helping you get greater consistently.

I might be youthful, however consistently I become more grounded in some new way.

Day 142
Always With You

(When thou passest through the waters, I will be with thee; and through the rivers, they shall not overflow thee; when thou walkest through the fire, thou shall not be burned; neither shall the flame kindle upon thee. Isaiah 43:2)

It would be decent if being a piece of God's family implied that everything in your life would dependably be great. Be that as it may, everybody has not really culminate times. At the point when your life appears to be not as much as flawless, recollect that God is with you. He guarantees that regardless of how intense or terrifying life gets, he'll be there. It's incredible to have an immaculate companion like God. God is with me when difficulties are out of hand, He comforts me and stop.

Day 143
Promises For A Lifetime

(And even to your old age I am he; and even to hoar hairs will I carry you; I have made, and I will hear; even I will carry, and will deliver you. Isaiah 46:4)

It may be difficult to envision now, however sometime you might be a grandmother or a grandpa. What do you think you'll look like at that point? Will you have silver hair? Or, then again a wrinkly face! You'll change a considerable measure as you become more seasoned; yet one thing will never show signs of change. God, who adores you so much right now, will continue cherishing you each day of your life.

Notwithstanding when I develop old and dim, God will even now stroll with me consistently.

Day 144
My Hiding Place

(And he hath made my mouth like a sharp sword; in the shadow of his hand hath he hid me, and made me a pointed shaft; in his quiver hath he hid me. Isaiah 49:2)

Do you have a most loved place to hide away? It's enjoyable to have a mystery spot behind a seat or under the bed or out in the yard. You can go there when you need to feel protected or simply be without anyone else. God is a sheltered place for us as well. His adoration resembles an immense cover we can wrap ourselves in. We can give God a chance to deal with us and protect us. When you can't hurried to your mystery put, recall that you can discover shield by imploring God whenever, wherever. I have a hiding spot nobody can see, God's affection will securely and unquestionably shroud me.

Day 145
The Best Love Of All

(Can a woman forget her sucking child, that she should not have compassion on the son of her womb? Yea, they may forget, yet will I not forget thee. Isaiah 49:15)

Have you at any point been isolated from your mother or father at the zoo or shopping center or library or wherever? Its startling, would you say it isn't? Yet, it's significantly scarier for your folks, who cherish you. Your mother doesn't need anything awful to transpire. Your father does all that he can to guard you. Be that as it may, as much as they cherish you, God adores you significantly more. Much the same as your folks, God thinks about all that you do. Furthermore, he won't ever given you a chance to out of his sight. God never forgets me all alone. He's dependably with me wherever I wander.

Day 146
A Shining Light

(And if I draw out my soul to the hungry, and satisfy the afflicted soul, then shall thy light rise in obscurity, and thy darkness be in the noonday. Isaiah 58:10)

When you were an infant, you required a considerable measure of assistance. However, the more established you get, the more you can help other people. On the off chance that your sister or sibling scratch their knee, you can help put a Band-Aid on it. In the event that a companion doesn't have any lunch, you can share yours. Helping other people is a great approach to share the light of God's affection. How might you help somebody today? I can help in case you're in a bad position. I'll be there as soon as humanly possible pronto!

Day 147
Just Like A Flower

(And the LORD shall guide thee continually, and satisfy thy soul in drought, and make fat thy bones; and thou shalt be like a watered garden, and like a spring of water, whose waters fail not. Isaiah 58:11)

Spring is an awesome time of year. Lovely blossoms fly up all over the place! Be that as it may, blossoms can't develop without great soil, heaps of daylight, and delicate rain. God made blossoms and the dirt, sun, and rain to enable them to develop. Like blossoms, we additionally require the great things God offers us to enable us to develop; great nourishment, warm apparel, families, and companions. Whenever you see a blossom; consider what God has done to enable you to develop as well.

Much the same as the blooms that develop from little seeds, God dependably gives me the things that I require.

Day 148
You're Delightful!

(Thou shalt no more be termed Forsaken; neither shall thy land any more be termed Desolate: but thou shalt be called Hephzibah, and thy Beulah: for the LORD delighteth in thee, and thy land shall be married. Isaiah 62:4)

Of the considerable number of things God influenced, individuals to make him the most joyful! God "savors the experience of you." That implies he is brimming with euphoria at whatever point he considers you. Notwithstanding when you do things you shouldn't, notwithstanding when you're in a terrible mind-set, notwithstanding when you aren't supposing him, he's reasoning about you.

I am God's kid and he supposes I am perfect. He takes a gander at me with awesome love and joy.

Day 149
God Always Knows

(And it shall come to pass, that before they call, I will answer; and while they are yet speaking, I will hear. Isaiah 65:24)

You don't generally know what your mother or father is arranging until the point that they let you know, isn't that right? Also, you don't know whether somebody needs your assistance unless he or she asks you. In any case, regardless of what's happening in your life right this moment. God definitely thinks about it. On the off chance that you have an issue, he definitely knows how to settle it. In case you're feeling awful, he's now figuring out how to enable you to rest easy. God knows you so well that he deals with your necessities previously you even ask him!

Before I call you, God, you're as of now there. You realize what I need, and I realize that you give it a second thought.

Day 150
Heavenly Hugs

(As one whom his mother comfortheth, so will comfort you; and ye shall be conforted in Jerusalem. Isaiah 66:13)

Mothers and fathers are decent at improving you feel when you're dismal. What's more, the Bible says God resembles a parent. He's somebody you can go to at whatever point you require an embrace or need somebody to hear you out. Also, much the same as your mother or father dependably tries to comfort you, God keeps you protected and secure. You can simply swing to him. He's happy to offer assistance.

My mother and my father give me heaps of affection, And even God gives me hugs from above!

Day 151
Special Delivery

(Before I formed thee in the belly I knew thee; and before thou camest forth out of the womb I sanctified thee, and I ordained thee a prophet unto the nations. Jeremiah 1:5)

Have your folks enlightened you concerning the day you joined their family? About how energized they were the point at which they held you for the first run through? What's more, simply think, God thoroughly understood you even before you took your first breath or cried your first tear; God cherished you. He arranged a great life for you. Also, he'll be paying special mind to you until the end of time.

Before I was conceived, God thought about me. He's cherished me perpetually and arranged what I'll be.

Day 152
The Right Path

(Thus saith the LORD, Stand ye in the ways, and see, and ask for the old paths, ye shall find rest for your souls. Buat they said, We will not walk therein. Jeremiah 6:16)

We as a whole settle on heaps of decisions amid the day. Some are simple, such as choosing which grain to have for breakfast. Others are hard, such as choosing whether to enlighten your folks reality regarding who broke the light. When you don't realize what to do, think about what God says. He instructs us to tell him and make the wisest decision. When we do, we can unwind and know we've settled on the correct decision.

When I should pick between wrong or right, God will help me to see the light.

Day 153
On Your Side

(Thy words were found, and I did eat them; and thy word was unto me the joy and rejoicing of mine heart; for I am called by thy name, o LORD God of hosts. Jeremiah 15:16)

This verse was composed by a man named Jeremiah. He composed it when he was feeling tragic and alone. He had loads of foes and not very many companions. Yet, notwithstanding when he felt loathsome, he recalled that God was his ally. Since he was God's tyke, he knew God was with him, notwithstanding amid a troublesome time. Furthermore, this made Jeremiah cheerful. Keep in mind forget God is your ally.

I'm upbeat to know God is dependably with me. Near to my side he has guaranteed to be!

Day 154
Something New

(Blessed is the man that trusteth in the LORD, and whose hope the LORD is. Jeremiah 17:7)

For whatever length of time that you live, you'll never come up short on new things to learn. You won't be the best at everything, except that ought to never prevent you from attempting. Notwithstanding when you're not exactly beyond any doubt how to accomplish something, you can make sure that God is with you. Regardless of the possibility that you don't find the ball or sing the correct note or compose the letter A consummately, God supposes you're awesome. You may not do everything right, particularly the first run through. Yet, God adores you notwithstanding. When I attempt new things, I won't not succeed, But rather God's perpetual love is all that I require.

Day 155
Your Exciting Future

(For I know the thoughts that I think toward you, saith the LORD, thoughts of peace, and not of evil, to give you an expected end. Jeremiah 29:11)

You won't not contemplate your future, but rather God's as of now got huge plans for you. You may be a specialist, a craftsman, or an educator when you grow up. In any case, whatever you do, God simply need you to tail him. He needs you to impart his adoration to the general population you get as you become together. He needs you to use sound judgment and remain nearby to him. When you do, you'll be carrying on with your life simply the way he needs you to.

I need to take after God's awesome arrangement. In the event that I do what he lets me know, I realize that I can!

Day 156
Calling On God

(Then shall ye call upon me, and ye shall go and pray unto me, and I will hearken unto you. Jeremiah 29:12)

Supplication is a smidgen like conversing with your grandmother on the phone. You can't see her, however you know she's there in light of the fact that you can hear her voice. When you implore God, you can't see him either. You may think about whether he's truly there. This verse is God's guarantee to you that he's constantly prepared to tune in. Despite the fact that you can't see God, converse with him. Reveal to him what's happening in your life. He cherishes to get notification from you. God dependably tunes in to me when I ask. I want to converse with him consistently.

Day 157
Just Look

(And ye shall seek me, and find me, when ye shall search for me with all your heart. Jeremiah 29:13)

In the event that you ever ponder where God is, check out you. You can't really observe God. In any case, on the off chance that you truly focus, you'll see him. Simply take a gander at a butterfly vacillating by and you'll see God's astonishing inventiveness. Or, then again tune in to a rainstorm and you'll hear God's energy. Feel a warm embrace from somebody you adore and you'll feel God's adoration, as well. God truly is appropriate here with us. We should simply look.

God's adoration encompasses me in blossoms and trees, In individuals and rainstorms, in bullfrogs and honey bees!

Day 158
God's Promise

(And ye shall be my people, and I will be your God. Jeremiah 30:22)

Long prior, God made an uncommon guarantee that can never be broken. He said we will dependably be his kin and he will dependably be our God. All through the Bible, individuals did things they shouldn't, however God still cherished them. We as a whole commit errors consistently, however God still cherishes us. God has stayed faithful to his obligation since the very beginning. We will be God's kin and he will be our kind, cherishing God always. That is a guarantee!

God made a guarantee he never will break.
He'll adore us everlastingly, whatever it takes.

Day 159
Everlasting Love

(The LORD hath appeared of old unto me, saying, Yea, I have loved thee with an everlasting love: therefore with lovingkindness have I drawn thee. Jeremiah 31:3)

Who do you adore (love) most? Your folks? Your most loved toy? Your puppy? When you truly adore somebody, it doesn't make a difference on the off chance that they hurt your sentiments once in a while or commit errors. You adore them at any rate. That is the manner by which God feels about you. His affection for you is strong to the point that it will keep going forever. He'll cherish you when you hurt his emotions. He'll adore you when you commit errors. He'll cherish you each day of your life!

God's adoration for me will never end. I'm so happy he's my companion.

Day 160
God Is Near

(Then shall the virgin rejoice in the dance, both young men and old together; for I will turn their mourning into joy, and will comfort them, and make them rejoice from their sorrow. Jeremiah 31:13)

Everybody experiences troublesome circumstances now and again. Be that as it may, God reveals to us that these troublesome circumstances won't keep going for long. On the off chance that your family is experiencing a hard time, recollect that God is with you and will comfort you. furthermore, recollect that sometime soon, God will take bliss back to your family. The terrible circumstances won't keep going forever; however God's adoration and care dependably will. Some days are fun, and some days are most certainly not. On a wide range of days, God cherishes me a ton!

Day 161
Nap Time

(For I have satiated the weary soul, and I have replenished every sorrowful soul. Jeremiah 31:25)

When you're truly tired, nothing feels superior to a decent little rest. Taking a rest amidst a bustling day can improve you feel to such an extent. Investing energy with God can resemble a little snooze for your heart. Regardless of whether you're chatting with God or simply getting a charge out of the world he made, your heart gets topped off with God's affection. You're brimming with vitality once more!

Sleeping gives me a new beginning. Chatting with God is a rest for my heart!

Day 162
Blue Skies

(Ah Lord God! Behold, thou hast made the heaven and the earth by thy great power and stretched out arm, and there is nothing too hard for thee: Jeremiah 32:17)

On a warm summer day, would it say it isn't pleasant to be outside with your companions? It's enjoyable to lie in the grass and gaze toward the blue sky and soft white mists. Is it accurate to say that it isn't astounding to consider God making such a lovely world? No one but God could be sufficiently capable to influence the sun and the totally open to sky. What's more, you get the chance to appreciate it all!

God, how could you make the sky so blue? You're so intense and great, as well!

Day 163
Just Ask

(Call unto me, and I will answer thee, and show thee great and mighty things, which thou knowest not. Jeremiah 33:3)

When you're eager, individuals give you nourishment, isn't that right? When you're drained, they most likely enable you to locate a comfortable place to rest. At whatever point you require something, you can approach somebody who watches over offer assistance. They'll offer it to you! That is the manner by which God is as well. Nobody thinks about you more than he does! When we require his assistance with a major or little issue, we should simply inquire.

God will help you-simply call him! He deals with issues, the huge and the little.

Day 164
Power When You Need It

(Their Redeemer is strong; the LORD of hosts is his name: he shall thoroughly plead their cause, that he may give rest to the land, and disquiet the inhabitants of Babylon. Jeremiah 50:34)

When you're youthful, you don't have much control over what transpires. Your folks choose what you should wear; what you ought to eat, and where you ought to go. More established children may state you can't play with them since you're not sufficiently solid to toss the ball or sufficiently quick to circled the bases. In any case, notwithstanding when you're youthful, you have God on your side. You won't not have much power alone, but rather God has enough for both of you!

Day 165
Lots Of Love

(It is of the LORD'S mercies that we are not consumed, because his compassions fail not. Lamentations 3:22)

When you get stuck in an unfortunate situation, you may figure your folks don't love you any longer. In any case, notwithstanding when they're angry with you, your mother and father love you more than you can envision. The same is valid for God. Notwithstanding when you do things you shouldn't, God cherishes you. He'll pardon you when you ask him. Furthermore, he'll love constantly you.

God's affection for me continues endlessly. He even cherishes me when I foul up.

Day 166
Brand-New Day

(They are new every morning: great is thy faithfulness. Lamentations 3:23)

Consistently is a spic and span starting! The sun awakens and you wake up, as well. You're upbeat and raring to go. Simply think about all the fun things you may do! You may fly a kite in the recreation center, take your puppy for a walk, or go for a swim. Each new day is one to appreciate.

God's adoration for me is crisp each day. He adores to demonstrate me in a wide range of ways!

Day 167
A New Friend

(The LORD is good unto them that wait for him, to the woul that seeketh him. Lamentations 3:25)

On the off chance that you need to make new companions, you need to do a little work. You need to converse with individuals, get some information about themselves, and invest energy with them. Becoming more acquainted with God takes a little work as well. To truly develop near God, we have to converse with him frequently, discover more about him by perusing the Bible, and influence him to some portion of every day. When we do, he'll be our companion for eternity!

God, you are my absolute best companion. You'll be my companion until the end.

Day 168
The Holy Spirit

(And shall put my spirit in you, and ye shall live, and I shall place you in your own land: then shall ye know that I the LORD have spoken it, and performed it, saith the LORD. Ezekiel 37:14)

Since God can't be here on earth with us, he gave us an exceptional blessing called the Holy Spirit. The Holy Spirit causes us use sound judgment and encourages us take after God. The greater part of all, the Holy Spirit lives in our souls and causes us recall the amount God cherishes us. What a brilliant blessing!

The Holy is unique to me – God's affection is the thing that he encourages me see.

Day 169
Beautiful Things

(How great are his signs! And how mighty are his wonders! His Kingdom is an everlasting kingdom, and his dominion is from generation to generation. Daniel 4:3)

Everything God made – from raindrops and butterflies to kids like you – reveals to us something about God. Raindrops enable things to develop and demonstrate to us that God take great care of the things he made. Butterflies demonstrate to us that God has some good times making lovely things for us to appreciate. You are an update that God loves to bring new individuals into the world. Check out you. What else would you be able to find out about God?

From winged creatures that travel to angle that swim, All God made focuses me to him.

Day 170
The Eternal King

(I make a decree, That in every dominion of my kingdom men tremble and fear before the God of Daniel; for he is the living God, and stedfast for ever, and his kingdom that which shall not be destroyed, and his dominion shall be even unto the end. Daniel 6:26)

The Bible was composed a great many years back. In those days, Daniel, the man who composed this verse, had no clue that you would some time or another read his story to find out about God. Be that as it may, Daniel knew one thing without a doubt. He trusted God would in any case be in charge, even later on. Furthermore, he was correct. The God who helped Daniel is a similar God who causes you today. God's affection goes on for all eras. He's the ruler of individuals and countries.

Day 171
Forgive And Forget

(To the LORD our God belong mercies and forgivenesses, though we have rebelled against him. Daniel 9:9)

Have you at any point needed to excuse somebody? It is difficult. is it? At the point when your sister or sibling offends you or remnants something that has a place with you, it can truly make you furious. Be that as it may, when she or he says they're sad and makes a request to be excused, you have to do your best to pardon (forgive) them. Keep in mind, God pardons us each time we ask him to. Furthermore, when we excuse each other, it feels so much better!

I can pardon (forgive) when somebody harms me. I realize that is the way God needs me to be!

Day 172
A Sure Thing

(Then shall we know, if we follow on to know the Lord; his going forth is prepared as the morning; and he shall come unto us as the rain, as the latter and former rain unto the earth. Hosea 6:3)

The sun rises and sets every single day. What's more, springtime comes every last year. You can rely on these things happening. You can likewise dependably rely on God to stay faithful to his commitments. God is dependably who he says he is. Furthermore, he generally does what he says he'll do. Much the same as you can depend on the sun coming up each morning or the rain falling in the spring, you can rely on God to be with you each day of your life.

Much the same as the sun comes up every day, I know God is with me the distance.

Day 173
God Is Perfect

(I willl not execute the fierceness of mine anger, I will not return to destroy Ephraim: for

I am God, and not man; the Holy One in the midst of thee: and I will not enter into the city. Hosea 11:9)

We don't know everything about God, however we do realize that God is altogether different from individuals. Individuals commit errors, yet God is great. Individuals can be mean, yet God is constantly kind. Individuals get frantic at each other, however God dependably excuses us. Individuals now and then detest each other, yet God cherishes us until the end of time. Aren't you happy we have a God like that?

God is immaculate and adoring and great. The way that he demonstrations is the way that we should!

Day 174
The Tree Of Life

(Ephraim shall say, What have I to do any more with idols? I have heard him, and observed him: I am like a green fir tree. From me is thy fruit found. Hosea 14:8)

What does an apple tree resemble? It is brimming with green leaves-and now and then apples? This verse says that God resembles a tree. Also, far and away superior, not at all like genuine trees, he delivers natural product lasting through the year! That implies God gives us all that we require, each time we require it. An apple tree doesn't have any apples on it amid the winter. Be that as it may, God's affection and care never end.

God deals with my requirements consistently. Close to me I know he generally will remain.

Day 175
Follow God

(Who is wise, and he shall understand these things? Prudent, and he shalt know them? For the ways of the LORD are right, and the just shall walk in them: but the transgressors shall fall therein. Hosea 14:9)

As you get older, more seasoned; individuals may attempt to influence you to do things you know aren't right. Somebody may disclose to you it's alright to lie or take something that doesn't have a place with you. Other individuals may disclose to you that God's principles are too difficult to take after or that they don't make a difference. Be that as it may, those individuals aren't right. The standards God gives us are there to ensure us. When we comply with God's guidelines, we're following the correct pioneer.

God, your tenets are generally that I require. I need to take afterwherever you lead.

Day 176
Let It Rain

(Be glad then, ye children of Zion, and rejoice in the LORD your God: for he hath given you the former rain moderately, and he will cause to come down for you the rain, the former rain, and the latter rain in the first month. Joel 2:23)

You may consider rain a blessing from God, particularly when you need to play outside. In any case, rain is a blessing we can't survive without. On the off chance that it never rained, we wouldn't have apples or strawberries or oranges. We wouldn't have drain to drink (bovines need to eat grass to make drain). We wouldn't have bread to eat (it's made out of wheat that develops on ranches). We wouldn't have garments to wear (garments are once in a while produced using cotton, which develops in fields). The rain drops out of the sky, I thank you, God, for the present I know why.

Day 177
Forever With God

(And it shall come to pass, that whosoever shall call upon the name of the LORD shall he delivered: for in mount Zion and in Jerusalem shall be deliverance, as the Lord hath said, and in the remnant whom the LORD shall call. Joel 2:32)

Once in a while people imagine that following God is a great deal of work. They think you need to do and say all the correct things and carry on with an ideal life to get to paradise. In any case, God says all we have to do to live with him always is request that he be with us. When we confide in God to administer to us, we are revealing to him that we cherish him – and that we need him to be the most essential piece of our life. So take after God. It's simple!

Going through everlastingly with God is no assignment. On the off chance that I need him to save me, I simply need to inquire.

Day 178
Run Away

(Seek good, and not evil, that ye may live: and so the LORD, the Gode of hosts, shall be with you, as ye have spoken. Amos 5:14)

Do you know what temptation is? It's needing to accomplish something you know you shouldn't, care for taking the last treat when you told your sister or sibling could have it. God knows we confront temptation consistently. His recommendation! Run! When you feel enticed to accomplish something you shouldn't, make tracks in an opposite direction from the allurement as quick as possible. With God's assistance, you can continue making the best decision. When I confront temptation, I simply flee. God dependably causes me to take after his way.

Day 179
A Whale Of A Tale

(And said, I cried by reason of mine affliction unto the LORD, and he heard me; out of the belly of hell cried I, and thou heardest my voice. Jonah 2:2)

Jonah was a man who got himself into huge trouble. At the point when Jonah didn't obey God, he wound up got in a tempest while he was out on a vessel. Far more detestable, he was tossed over the edge and gulped by a vast fish! However, even after all that, Jonah knew he could put stock in God to help him. He solicited God to take mind from him, and God did. He got Jonah out of the fish and protected him. in the event that God can deal with Jonah, he can deal with you, as well.

When I'm in a bad position, God realizes what to do. He protected Jonah. He'll safeguard me, as well!

Day 180
Finding Your Way

(The breaker is come up before them; they have broken up, and have passed through the gate, and are gone out by it; and their king shall pass before them, and the LORD on the head of them. Micah 2:13)

You've been hearing a ton about after God and living the way he needs you to. In case you don't know how to do that, don't stress. Give God a chance to help you. Read the Bible, take to him, and tune in for his voice in your heart. God will never abandon you all alone. He'll be appropriate close to you consistently, helping you discover your direction.

At whatever point I battle to discover my direction, God ensures that I don't stray.

Day 181
Growing Up

(For all people will walk every one in the name of his god, and we will walk in the name of the LORD our God for ever and ever. Micah 4:5)

As you grow up, loads of things about you will change. You'll appear to be unique, you'll live in an alternate house, and you may even have an alternate last name sometime in the not so distant future. Be that as it may, regardless of the amount you change, one thing will dependably remain the same. God will dependably be with you. Notwithstanding when you head out to school or get hitched or turn into a grandparent, God will be there keeping an eye out for you and dealing with you.

Regardless of the amount I will change as I develop, God will remain with me always I know!

Day 182
Help At Hand

(Therefore I will look unto the LORD; I will wait for the God of my salvation: my God will hear me. Micah 7:7)

When you require enable, you to can discover it in bunches of spots. Your folks can help you, and your companions. furthermore, your educator, as well. Be that as it may, there will be times when it appears there's nobody around to offer assistance. That is the reason it's so essential to have God in your life. He's with all of you the time. He can help at whatever point you require him.

I can get assistance from the general population I know, And God's likewise with me wherever I go.

Day 183
Night And Day

(I will bear the indignation of the LORD, because I have sinned against him, until he plead my cause, and execute judgment for me: he will bring me forth to light, and I shall behold his righteousness. Micah 7:9)

When you're wiped out with an icy cold, it can appear like it will never end. Or, on the other hand when you wake up frightened amidst the night, you may think about whether the sun will ever come up. Be that as it may, much the same as the night dependably transforms into day, awful circumstances in the end transform into great circumstances. In case you're experiencing serious difficulties at this moment, request that God enable you to traverse it. He'll comfort you until the point when you feel radiant once more!

Similarly as the sun replaces the moon, I realize that great days will return again soon.

Day 184
A Good Place

(The LORD is good, a strong hold in the day of trouble; and he knoweth them that trust in him. Nahum 1:7)

Doesn't it feel great to snuggle with your mother? Or, on the other hand twist up on your bed with your most loved toy? Don't you cherish holding your father's hand when you're out for a walk? Whatever you do, ensure you swing to God, as well. God guarantees to dependably be your shelter a protected place.

God will enable me to feel protected and warm. He shields me from a wide range of damage.

Day 185
A Starry Sky

(O LORD, I have heard thy speech, and was afraid; O LORD, revive thy work in the midst of the years, in the midst of the years make known; in wrath remember mercy. Habakkuk 3:2)

The night sky is truly astonishing. It's loaded with shimmering stars, zooming meteors, and obviously the huge, splendid moon. Also, God is the person who framed each one of those zillions of stars and every one of the planets. He made the meteors and the moon. As you gaze toward the profound, dull sky this evening, say a supplication. Much obliged to you God for his brilliant creation. It's his blessing to you.

The stars in the sky twinkle brilliantly every night, Reminding me of God's profound love and enjoyment.

Day 186
Climbing High

(The LORD God is my strength, and he will make my feet like hinds' feet, and he will make me to walk upon mine high places. To the chief singer on my stringed instruments. Habakkuk 3:19)

Have you at any point seen a deer running in a field? Deer can run rapidly and effectively finished fields and even mountains. When you have a hard day, it resembles a mountain that is difficult to move over. This verse says God will enable us to climb the "mountains" that appear in our lives. With God next to us, we can be as effortless as deer!

No heap of inconvenience is too high for me. God encourages me run like a deer, you see!

Day 187
Love Songs

(The LORD thy God in the midst of thee is mighty; he will save, he will rejoice over thee with joy; he will rest in his love, he will joy over thee with singing. Zephaniah 3:17)

God adores (loves) it when you sing a melody to him. Yet, did you realize that God sings to you, as well? God adores (loves) you so much that occasionally he can't resist the urge to sing a melody to you! His melody may seem like flying creatures twittering in the trees or a delicate breeze blowing through the takes off. It may seem like rain or waterfall or crickets tweeting during the evening. Each stable is an affection tune straight from God's heart to you.

I hear God singing to me all around, From the trees to the lake to the serene night air.

Day 188
Wherever You Go

(And I will strengthen them in the LORD, and they shall walk up and down in his name, saith the LORD. Zechariah 10:12)

Your life will take you bunches of fascinating spots. You may visit a companion in an alternate state. You could visit another nation sometime in the not so distant future. What's more, regardless of where you go, you'll discover God there. You could go to the opposite side of the world, and God would be there. You could go to the abandon, the mountains, or the sea and still discover God appropriate close by. Wherever you are, God is there as well.

Alone in the betray or out on the ocean, God will be there, continually watching over me.

Day 189
Since The Very Beginning

(For I am the LORD, I change not, therefore ye sons of Jacob arre not consumed. Malachi 3:6)

When you hear energizing stories from the Bible, possibly you think about whether God still watches over individuals the way he did every one of those years back. The appropriate response is yes! Much the same as God helped Noah get away from the Great Flood and helped Jonah make due in the stomach of a major fish, God ensures you today. Much the same as he excused King David for his mix-ups and remained with the general population of Israel notwithstanding when they played Judas on God, God pardons you today. God has cherished and tended to his kin since the very beginning. Furthermore, he will love and administer to you until the end of time!

God is the same, yesterday, and tomorrow, He's dependably with us in happiness and in distress.

Day 190
Don't Wait!

(And saying, Repent ye: for the kingdom of heaven is at hand. Matthew 3:2)

When you meet another companion you truly like, it is senseless to state, "I would prefer not to be companions now. We should hold up until we're more established." If you did, you'd pass up a major opportunity for some incredible circumstances! A similar thing is valid with God. Some of the time individuals figure they don't have to invest energy with God until they're more established. Be that as it may, id we hold up to be companions with God, we'll pass up a great opportunity for his uncommon love, his assistance, and his kinship. So don't hold up – be God's companion today!

Day 191
Look On The Bright Side

(Blessed are they that mourn: for they shall be comforted. Matthew 5:4)

Everybody feels miserable now and again. In any case, God cherishes us so much that he generally discovers approaches to improve us feel. Our folks embrace us and wipe away our tears. Our companions influence us to snicker and play with us when we're desolate. The daylight pursues away desolate mists. Whenever you feel dismal, look on the splendid side. What's fulfilling you feel once more?

On the off chance that things look miserable from your perspective, Remember to look on the brilliant side as well!

Day 192
Doing What's Right

(Blessed are they which do hunger and thirst after righteousness: for they shall be filled. Matthew 5:6)

What might you do if a companion instructed you to accomplish something incorrectly? Making the wisest decision isn't generally simple. Individuals may ridicule you or reveal to you you're unusual. In any case, when you make the best decision, you're additionally doing the best thing. Doing what's wrong prompts inconvenience. Making the right decision will dependably make you glad at last. You feel great when you know you're doing what God needs you to do.

It feels so great to make the wisest decision – To take after God with the greater part of your strength.

Day 193
A Pure Heart

(Blessed are the pure in heart: for they shall see God. Matthew 5:8)

The Bible says that you will be glad on the off chance that you have an unadulterated heart. Having an unadulterated heart implies you see the positive qualities in other individuals and occasions. For example, if it's a stormy day, a man with an unadulterated heart realizes that God sent the rain to enable the blooms to develop. In the event that a companion is in a terrible temperament, a man with an unadulterated heart sees past her or his companion's crankiness to the pity he may be feeling. Request that God give you the gift of an unadulterated heart.

With a heart that is unadulterated, I can see
All the decency encompassing me!

Day 194
The Greatest Prize Of All

(Rejoice, and be exceeding glad: for great is your reward in heaven; for so persecuted they the prophets which were before you. Matthew 5:12)

On the off chance that somebody requesting that you portray paradise, what might state? Do you believe it's a place loaded with blessed messengers, soft white mists, and roads of gold? The Bible doesn't let us know precisely what paradise will resemble. Be that as it may, it says that the individuals who have faith in Jesus will live there always with God. Notwithstanding when life is intense, we can anticipate the best prize of all – HEAVEN!

Life here on earth is quite recently the starting, Heaven's the prize we would all be able to be winning!

Day 195
Love For Everyone

(But I say unto you, Love your enemies, bless them that curse you, do good to them that hate you, and pray for them which despitefully use you, and persecute you; Matthew 5:44)

Of the considerable number of things God requests that we do, cherishing (loving) an adversary (enemy)is one of the hardest. How might you cherish a man you don't care for? How might you appeal to God for somebody who harms you? That is the place God comes in. Request that he give you additional affection in your heart. At that point you can be benevolent to individuals who aren't thoughtful to you. Who knows-you may even move toward becoming companions!

Albeit cherishing others can some of the time be extreme, God fills me with affection that is all that anyone could need.

Day 196
Beautiful Flowers

(Wherefore, if God so clothe the grass of the field, which today is, and tomorrow is cast into the oven, shall he not much more clothe you, O ye of little faith? Matthew 6:30)

Summer is the ideal opportunity for blossoms! Whenever you're riding in an auto, attempt to see all the lovely wildflowers developing in favor of the street or in the fields. Those plants don't have a place with anybody, so it's dependent upon God to enable them to develop. How? He ensures they have all the rain and daylight they require. Also, God looks after you, as well significantly more than he watches over the plants. When you see delightful blooms, recollect how God tends to them – and for you, as well! God, you watch over every one of the blooms I see. You enable them to develop, Just like you help me!

Day 197
From Day To Day

(But seek ye first the kingdom of God, and his righteousness; and all these things shall be added unto you. Matthew 6:33)

God guarantees to give you what you require from everyday. Perhaps you don't have the same number of toys as you'd like. Possibly some of your companions appear to have significantly more than you do. Regardless of the possibility that you like the toys you have, there dependably is by all accounts some new toy that you think you require. Be that as it may, God needs you to be content with what you have. You may not generally get all that you need, but rather you can make certain you'll generally have what you require.

God, you give me all that I require. Your affection (love) for me is ensured!

Day 198
One Day At A Time

(Take therefore no though for the morrow; for the morrow shall take thought for the things of itself. Sufficient unto the day is the evil thereof. Matthew 6:34)

Life is intended to be lived each day by itself. Be that as it may, it's simple for individuals particularly adults! – to overlook this. Rather than appreciating today, they're as of now agonizing over what they'll do tomorrow. In any case, today is brimming with superb minutes, and God needs us to appreciate every day completely. So don't stress over tomorrow. Appreciate today! Today is so loaded with great things to see, That tomorrow can simply sit tight for me.

Day 199
Hidden Treasure

(For every one that asketh receiveth; and he that seeketh findeth; and to him that knocketh it shall be opened. Matthew 7:8)

Imagine you are going on a fortune chase. You have a guide and a rundown of signs to enable you to seek. You're altogether energized, yet then you experience serious difficulties finding the fortune. Does that influence you to need to stop? Possibly. However, the Bible says that in the event that you continue seeking, you'll find what you're searching for at last. So whether you're searching for covered fortune or endeavoring to discover answers to questions you have about God, never surrender!

On the off chance that you don't surrender, you'll think that its actual

The appropriate responses you need will come to you.

Day 200
Good Things

(If ye then, being evil, know how to give good gifts unto your children, how much more shall your Father which is in heaven give good things to them that ask him? Matthew 7:11)

When you approach your mother and father for something great, they will do all that they can to ensure you get it. In the event that you disclose to them you're frosty, they'll give you a warm cover. When you're eager, they'll give you a warm cover. When you're ravenous, they'll ensure you enough to eat. God is a great deal like your folks. He adores to give you great things when you request them. You never must fear approaching God for the great things you require. I Talk to God, and he hears what I say. He addresses every one of my issues every moment, every day.

Day 201
Live And Love

(Therefore all things whatsoever ye would that men should do to you, do ye even so to them; for this is the law and the prophets. Matthew 7:12)

How does God want you to live? Simply recollect this verse. God needs you to treat others the way you'd jump at the chance to be dealt with. When you see somebody who needs assistance, give him a hand. When somebody converses with you, tune in to what he or she says. Give embraces, be caring, and show individuals the sort of affection you get a kick out of the chance to be appeared.

On the off chance that my companions needs some assistance and I happen to see, I'll help him the way I'd need him to help me.

How does God need you to live? Simply recollect this verse. God needs you to treat others the way you'd jump at the chance to be dealt with. When you see somebody who needs assistance, give him a hand. When somebody converses with you, tune in to what he or she says. Give embraces, be caring, and show individuals the sort of affection you get a kick out of the chance to be appeared. On the off chance that my companions needs some assistance and I happen to see, I'll help him the way I'd need him to help me.

Day 202
Solid Ground

(Therefore whosoever heareth these sayings of mine, and doeth them, I will liken him unto a wise man, which built his house upon a rock; Matthew 7:24)

Have you at any point manufactured a sand stronghold? They're enjoyable to assemble, right? They look awesome, however they don't generally keep going long. A decent, solid wave will thump them over. On the off chance that you need to assemble something that endures, you have to utilize more grounded materials than sand. God says we should assemble our lives on something solid as well his educating in the Bible. Tuning in to God is much the same as building a house on strong shake as opposed to moving sand.

When I tune in to God, I'm on strong ground. I'll be shrewd regardless of what comes around.

Day 203
You're Worth It!

(Fear ye not therefore, ye are of more value than many sparrows. Matthew 10:31)

God dependably takes great care of his creation. He ensures every one of the creatures have spots to live. What's more, when a creature gets hurt, God thinks about it. He even notification when a little winged animal drops out of its home or a bunny needs sustenance. Be that as it may, the Bible says he minds much more in regards to you. In the event that he takes such great care of creatures, simply think how intently he's viewing over you! God administers to the chipmunks and feathered creatures that I see. In any case, I discover he thinks much more about me!

Day 204
A Light Load

(For my yoke is easy, and my burden is light. Matthew 11:30)

When you're youthful and your legs are short, you get drained out more rapidly than somebody taller does. Exactly when you figure you can't walk another progression, somebody lifts you up and conveys you. Aren't you happy? Somebody greater and more grounded than you doesn't might suspect you are substantial by any stretch of the imagination. God is the greatest, most grounded individual in the universe. What's more, he needs us to turn over every one of our stresses and considerations to him. Our stresses are too substantial for us, yet they are a light load for God!

God knows my stresses are too overwhelming for me. He'll convey them all with the goal that I can be free.

Day 205
Like A Child

(Whosoever therefore shall humble himself as this little child, the same is greatest in the kingdom of heaven. Matthew 18:4)

Heaps of children can hardly wait to be more established. They need to be taller or more astute or more grounded so they can do every one of the things adults do. Be that as it may, God says adults ought to be more similar to kids! Kids are typically all the more trusting. They trust God will deal with every one of their needs. They know God is with them. Yet, at times adults overlook those things. As you grow up, bear in mind every one of the lessons you've found out about God. There's nothing adolescent about believing him. As little and youthful as I may be, It's actual that adults can gain from me!

Day 206
Time With God

(For where two or three are gathered together in my name, there am I in the midst of them. Matthew 18:20)

Do you know why individuals go to church? A major reason is that it is where we can be with God. However, there are numerous different spots to make the most of God's quality as well. When you and your family supplicate before supper, God is there. When you play outside with a companion on the planet God made, God is there. When you sing a melody about God or express gratitude toward him for all the immense things he's given you, God is there. So when you need to invest energy with God, get a companion. At that point welcome God to go along with you!

I can invest energy with God anyplace. Whatever I do, he'll generally be there.

Day 207
Believe It!

(And all things, whatsoever ye shall ask in prayer, believing, ye shall receive. Matthew 21:22)

When you approach God for something, what do you figure he does? Does he disregard you? Does he hold up to check whether you merit what you've requested? No. When you approach God for something, he hears you. The best part is that he guarantees to reply. When you supplicate, approach God for the things you truly require. At that point believe him to give you what you request even in startling ways!

When I converse with God, he tunes in and cares. I can put stock in God to answer my petitions.

Day 208
Small Things

(His lord said unto him, Well done, thou good and faithful servant: thou hast been faithful over a few things, I will make thee ruler over many things: enter thou into the joy of thy lord. Matthew 25:21)

Jesus recounted his companions a tale about a man who went on a long outing. Before he cleared out, he gave each of his workers an alternate occupation to do. A few occupations were huge and some were little. When he returned, he was exceptionally satisfied with the hireling who did his little occupation well. Keep in mind this story when your folks give you employments to do. When you do even little employments well, your folks will have the capacity to believe you more. Perhaps they'll say you can ride your bicycle down the piece or remain overnight with a companion!

I'll demonstrate my folks that they can believe me. I'll do all I'm asked, and afterward they will see and be happy.

Day 209
Do It For Jesus

(And the king shall answer and say unto them, Verily I say unto you, Inasmuch as ye have done it unto one of the least of these my brethren, ye have done it unto me. Matthew 25:40)

Jesus is God's Son. When he lived on earth, he demonstrated to individuals best practices to take after God. Something he instructed is that we have to treat everybody the way we would treat him. In the event that you saw Jesus sitting alone at a play area, you'd go converse with him. In the event that you saw that Jesus was tragic or frightened or harmed, you'd endeavor to help him.

Jesus said we have to do likewise for the general population around us. At whatever point we indicate love to one of God's kin, we're demonstrating affection to God, as well.

When I help a man who's terrified or feels blue, It's much the same as I'm helping Jesus, as well.

Day 210
You Can Be Sure

(Teaching them to observe all things whatsoever I have commanded you: and lo, I am with you always, even unto the end of the world. Amen. Matthew 28:20)

At the point when Jesus left the earth to run live in paradise with God, his Father, he made a guarantee to every one of his companions on earth. He said he'd be with them for eternity. What's more, that is not the first occasion when that sort of guarantee was made. God made a similar guarantee to us toward the start of the Bible, before Jesus came to live on earth. Why did God give us that guarantee twice? To ensure we realize that God, our Father, and Jesus, his Son, are dependably with us. Together they, alongside God's Spirit, ensure us, answer our supplications, pardon our oversights when we say we are sad, and demonstrate to us their affection.

To know God is with me is constantly decent,
The Bible says so not once, but rather twice!

Day 211
Going Fishing

(And Jesus said unto them, Come ye after me, and I will make you to become fishers of men. Mark 1:17)

On the off chance that you've at any point gone fishing, you know you require snare something the fish need to find anything. The same is valid for enlightening individuals concerning God. When we share God's affection with others, they'll feel so great that they'll need to find out about him. You don't need to do anything unique to inform individuals concerning God. Simply cherish them and think about them. Furthermore, before you know it, they'll be snared!

When you take a gander at my life, I trust you will see The affection for God sparkling brilliantly through me.

Day 212
A Doctor's Touch

(When Jesus heard it, he saith unto them, they that are whole have no need of the physican, but they that are sick: I came not to call the righteous, but sinners to repentance. Mark 2:17)

How would you feel when you have a sore throat and a fever? Awful, isn't that so? When you're wiped out, you-and your folks! – are happy your doctor knows only the correct prescription to improve your feeling. Jesus discloses to us that, much the same as a doctor, or a specialist, he came to enable the individuals who to require him. When you're wiped out, you require a specialist, a doctor. furthermore, when you understand you require offer assistance. Jesus is in that spot to excuse you and help you.

Prescription may influence you to feel great as new, But Jesus is the one forgiving you!

Day 213
Listen And Learn

(For he that hath, to him shall be given: and he that hath not, from him shall be taken even that which he hath. Mark 4:25)

Listening is a vital thing to do. Yet, it isn't generally simple. Some of the time your mother or father may state, "Offer your toys" when you don't have a craving for sharing. Or, on the other hand they may state, "Come clean" when you've quite recently committed an error. Yet, God says it's critical to tune in. Your folks can enable you to figure out how to take after God better. So when they talk, it's great to tune in and get it.

Guardians can show you what's privilege and what's off-base. They'll enable you to figure out how to get along.

Day 214
For His Sake

(For whosoever will save his life shall lose it; but whosoever shall lose his life for my sake and the gospel's, the same shall save it. Mark 8:35)

As you grow up you will find you can do numerous things. You may discover that you can compose stories. Or, then again paint pictures. Or, on the other hand sing delightfully. What's more, you'll need to utilize your abilities to end up plainly everything you can be. Be that as it may, recollect forget that your abilities are blessings from God. He needs you to utilize them to spread his adoration to his reality. What gifts do you have that you can impart to others today?

Whatever my blessings, they're all from God's hand. sharing his adoration through them will be so incredible! So Grand!

Day 215
Good Deeds

(For whosoever shall give you a cup of water to drink in my name, because ye belong to Christ, verily I say unto you, he shall not lose his reward. Mark 9:41)

Despite the fact that you are extremely youthful, you can have a major effect in the lives of people around you. At the point when your mother or father is drained, give them an embrace. At the point when your sister or sibling is tragic, sing her a tune. At the point when a companion needs a mate, welcome him or her to your home. Being benevolent to others satisfies God. What's more, it implies a great deal to the general population you think about.

Minding and sharing is the manner by which you should live. Attempt it and see exactly the amount you can give!

Day 216
Important To Jesus

(But when Jesus saw it, he was much displeased, and said unto them, Suffer the little children to come unto me, and forbid them not: for of such is the kingdom of God. Mark 10:14)

One day when Jesus lived on earth a few mothers and fathers conveyed their little youngsters to Jesus so he could favor them. Be that as it may, a few grown-ups figured the children shouldn't trouble Jesus. These grown-ups endeavored to send the children away. Be that as it may, how wrong the grown-ups were! Jesus let them know evidently that youngsters like you are vital to him. Why? Since you demonstrate to adults industry standards to love and put stock in God. Why not give that great blessing to the grown-ups around you? Jesus adores little youngsters like me. Trusting and cherishing is the best approach to be!

Day 217
Who's First

(But many that are first shall be last; and the last first. Mark 10:31)

Being imperative influences a few people to feel uncommon. They'll offend other people or cheat or mislead ensure they're first at everything. In any case, God's staggering adoration flips around all the world's standards. The general population who emerge to God are frequently not the ones who are notable here on earth. Rather, they are individuals who discreetly adore God more than whatever else. They think about others and are caring and insightful. Regardless of the possibility that you do wind up noticeably popular when you grow up, recollect forget what God believes is imperative. Attempt to be that sort of individual first.

In the event that you figure you should be first in line, Know that God's view is diverse now and again.

Day 218
A Special Baby

(And the angel answered and said unto her, The Holy Ghost shall come upon thee, and the power of the Highest shall overshadow thee: therefore also that holy thing which shall be born of thee shall be called the Son of God. Luke 1:35)

You've effectively found out about a portion of the extraordinary things Jesus did and said when he lived on earth. Be that as it may, Jesus was extraordinary even before he was conceived. Jesus' mom, Mary, discovered she would have a child when a heavenly attendant landed at her home and advised her. How energizing! The blessed messenger additionally disclosed to Mary that her child would be God's own Son. Now that is an entirely uncommon child! The heavenly attendant had something exceptional to state. God's own special Son was en route!

Day 219
True Faith

(And blessed is she that believed: for there shall be a performance of those things which were told her from the Lord. Luke 1:45)

The blessed messenger (angel) who went by Mary revealed to her that she was to be the mother of God's own Son. Mary got this news months before Jesus was prepared to be conceived. What's more, despite the fact that the blessed messenger's news was difficult to trust, Mary put stock in God. She held up persistently. At long last Jesus was conceived, and Mary was glad since she trusted God's guarantee.

Mary trusted the blessed messenger's(angel's) extraordinary news.

Trusting God is the best thing to pick.

Day 220
The Shepherd's Surprise

(And there were in the same country shepherds abiding in the field, keeping watch over their flock by night. And the angel said unto them, Fear not; for, behold, I bring you good tidings of great joy, which shall be to all people. For unto you is born this day in the city of David a Saviour, which is Christ the Lord. Luke 2:8, 10-11)

Would you be able to envision what those shepherds more likely than not felt like? They were out late around evening time viewing their sheep. They were likely worn out and frosty and perhaps somewhat exhausted. At that point, out of the blue, a heavenly attendant appeared! He gave them the most mind boggling news ever. God's Son, Jesus, had been conceived! At times we overlook exactly how astonishing it is that God thought enough about us to send his exclusive Son to live on earth with us. In any case, he did. What's more, that is truly a comment! Uplifting news came to them while they viewed their sheep. God's Son was conceived when most people were sleeping.

Day 221
Full Of Questions

(And it came to pass, that after three days they found him in the temple, sitting in the midst of the doctors, both hearing them, and asking them questions. And all that heard him were astonished at his understanding and answers. Luke 2:46-47)

At the point when Jesus was a young man, he presumably enjoyed a great deal of similar things you do, such as snickering and pursuing frogs and playing amusements with companions. He likewise got a kick out of the chance to learn, particularly about the things his brilliant Father was doing on the planet. So he conversed with God and to individuals who knew the appropriate responses, similar to educators and his folks. When you need to find out about God, do what Jesus did. Converse with the adults throughout your life. Solicit parts from questions!

God, there's so much I can think about you. On the off chance that I make inquiries, I'll recognize what is valid.

Day 222
Jesus As A Boy

(He hath put down the mighty from their seats, and exalted them of low degree. Luke 2:52)

Jesus was God's Son, so you'd think he'd be super shrewd and super solid. Be that as it may, Jesus was additionally a man, much the same as you. Perhaps he had pimples or hair that stuck up in amusing spots. Possibly he was timid or jump at the chance to peruse. We don't know much about Jesus' life as a kid. Yet, we do know he needed to tune in to his folks, figure out how to coexist with others, and do the various things kids need to do.

On the off chance that you feel alone here and there, recall that Jesus recognizes what it resembles to be a child. All things considered, he was youthful once as well. Jesus was youthful like me for some time. He realizes what It was like to be a child.

Day 223
Love Your Enemies

(But love ye your enemies, and do good, and lend, hoping for nothing again; and your reward shall be great, and ye shall be the children of the Highest: for he is kind unto the unthankful and to the evil. Luke 6:35)

Jesus showed his devotees another approach to treat individuals. Generally when individuals hurt you, you would prefer not to hurt them back. On the off chance that individuals don't care for you, you don't care for them either. However, Jesus instructs us to love our adversaries. It's never simple, yet Jesus can help you. In the event that you do great to your adversaries, you could change your life and theirs-eternity.

When somebody is mean, I implore that I'll discover Love in my heart and quality to be caring.

Day 224
Jesus' Example

(Judge not, and ye shall not be judged; condemn not, and ye shall not be condemned: forgive, and ye shall be forgiven: Luke 6:37)

How would you figure out how to do new things? Ordinarily it's by watching others. You can figure out how to ride a bicycle, play get, or even skip by watching another person do it and afterward attempting it yourself. It's a similar path with figuring out how to excuse individuals when they accomplish something incorrectly. We figure out how to excuse how Jesus pardoned others. The more you find out about how Jesus acted, the all the more lenient you'll be toward others.

Excusing is hard when somebody fouls up. In any case, I can watch Jesus and take after along.

Day 225
Filled With Light

(If thy whole body therefore be full of light, having no part dark, the whole shall be full of light, as when the bright shining of a candle doth give thee light. Luke 11:36)

It's practically difficult to remain inside on a bright day. A reasonable blue sky and loads of daylight essentially implore you to come join in the festivities. What's more, when individuals see the light of Jesus' affection radiating through you, they'll be attracted to you, as well. They'll need to know where all your joy and bliss originate from. You can reveal to them that when Jesus lives in your heart, consistently is loaded with daylight!

At the point when your heart is loaded with delight and love, You'll sparkle with light from God above.

Day 226
Too Many To Count!

(But even the very hairs of your head are all numbered. Fear not therefore: ye are of more value than many sparrows. Luke 12:7)

Do you know what amount of hair you have? Do your mother and father know? You could take a stab at tallying each and every hair on your head, however you'd never make sense of it. There are quite recently too much! In any case, God gives careful consideration to you that he knows what number of hairs you have. Furthermore, he knows everything else about you as well. Is it accurate to say that it isn't decent to have somebody think such a great amount about you?

In spite of the fact that I can't check the greater part of my hairs, They can advise me that God dependably minds.

Day 227
A Careful Search

(Either what woman having ten pieces of silver, if she lose one piece, doth not light a candle, and sweep the house, and seek diligently till she find it? Luke 15:8)

Doesn't it make you insane when you can't locate a most loved toy? You can't quit pondering it. You'll draw of the lounge chair pads, burrow through your storage room, even slither under your bed until the point when you discover your toy. God feels a similar route about us, however considerably more emphatically. We are on the whole imperative to him. At the point when God knows even one of us is lost or in a bad position or not tailing him, he looks for us until the point that we're securely home with him once more. In the event that you ever get lost, you soon will be found. God will ensure you remain protected and sound.

Day 228
A Tiny Seed

(And the Lord said, If ye had faith as a grain of mustard seed, ye might say unto this sycamine tree, Be thou planted in the sea: and it should obey you. Luke 17:6)

Jesus' supporters needed to know how they could have more confidence in God. So Jesus utilized a mustard seed for instance. Why a mustard seed? Since it's one of the most modest seeds around. However, it's alive and developing. At the point when it's planted in the ground, it starts to flourish and after that spread. Like the modest mustard seed, a little measure of confidence will flourish and become within you. Before long it will spread and will deliver great outcomes throughout your life. Express gratitude toward God for the minor seed of confidence developing in you!

My confidence may be little and difficult to see, But it's constantly alive and developing in me!

Day 229
Alive Again!

(He is not here, but is risen: remember how he spake unto you when he was yet in Galilee. Luke 24:6)

God the Father sent his Son, Jesus to live with us on earth. Jesus demonstrated to us generally accepted methods to love others and excuse the. He showed us how to be thoughtful to individuals who are not quite the same as But he additionally accomplished something truly astounding. Jesus was killed for the wrong things we've done, yet he didn't remain dead. God breathed life into him back once more.

God did this to demonstrate to us that Jesus us more effective than death! What's more, we can live perpetually in paradise with him as well in the event that we believe him and request that he pardon us.

God can do anything-yea, he can. He even made Jesus alive once more!

Day 230
From The Beginning

(In the beginning was the Word, and the Word was with God, and the Word was God. The same was in the beginning with God. John 1:1-2)

Keep in mind at the absolute starting point of this book where you read about God making the entire universe? Indeed, even path in those days, toward the get-go, Jesus was with God his Father in paradise. That implies Jesus thoroughly understands individuals' lives, from Adam and Eve on. He likewise knows the amount God adores us and nurtures us. What's more, he feels a similar way. Jesus wasn't only a man who lived on the earth for a little time. He's been around since the main day of time, and simply like God, he'll be with you until the last.

Much obliged to you, dear Jesus, for thinking about me. Nothing happens that you can't see.

Day 231
You Are Valuable

(For God so loved the world, that he gave his only begotten Son, that whosoever believeth in him should not perish, but have everlasting life. John 3:16)

When we truly need something, now and again we must surrender a considerable measure to get it. When something is that essential, we say it's "profitable." And in God's eyes, we are the most significant of all. So what did God offer up to ensure we could go through always with him in paradise? He surrendered his Son, Jesus. It more likely than not been hard for God to send us his Son, when he knew Jesus would need to bite the dust for the wrong things we've done. Be that as it may, he supposes we're justified, despite all the trouble!

God sent us his Son so we could live. What a brilliant present for God to give!

Day 232
Drink Up!

(But whosoever drinketh of the water that I shall give him shall never thirst; but the water that I shall give him shall be in him a well of water springing up into everlasting life. John 4:14)

What's the one thing each living animal needs to live? No. Not dessert. It's water! When we don't get enough water to drink, we get, extremely parched. That is the means by which our bodies remind us to continue drinking. Jesus said that tailing him and adoring him resembles drinking water. Much the same as we require water, we likewise require him to live. What's more, when we don't get enough of him, our hearts get anxious for his adoration.

On the off chance that you take after Jesus, he guarantees your heart will never be parched again.

Go to God's wellspring and you'll never thirst. He'll top you off. Simply put Jesus first!

Day 233
More Than Enough

(And Jesus took the loaves, and when he had given thanks, he distributed to the disciples, and the disciples to them that were set down, and likewise of the fishes as much as they would. John 6:11)

One day an immense horde of individuals came to tune in to Jesus. At the point when the general population got ravenous, Jesus' companions glanced around for some sustenance to give them. Be that as it may, the sum total of what they had was a couple of rolls of bread and a few fish. At that point something mind boggling happened. Some way or another Jesus transformed this little sum into enough sustenance to nourish a large number of individuals. What's more, they even had scraps! Jesus did a great deal of stunning things to indicate individuals that God would dependably deal with them.

At the point when Jesus gave the group a comment, A couple of rolls and fishes turned out to be a significant treat!

Day 234
The Brightest Light

(Then spake Jesus again unto them, saying, I am the light of the world: he that followeth me shall not walk in darkness, but shall have the light of life. John 8:12)

What's the brightest light you can consider? Spotlights are brilliant, and they can light substantial ranges.

Be that as it may, would you be able to envision a light sufficiently splendid to illuminate the entire world at one time? Jesus told his adherents that he was the Light of the world. He sparkles out to all individuals, demonstrating to them the best approach to genuine life. God's adoration is so solid and splendid that it illuminates the entire world. What's more, when you have God's affection living inside you, you can illuminate your edge of the world as well!

Jesus conveys light to the darkest of spots. His adoration is a light that will sparkle on our appearances.

Day 235
Listening For God's Voice

(To him the porter openeth; and the sheep hear his voice; and he calleth his own sheep by name, and leadeth them out. And when he putteth forth his own sheep, he goeth before them, and the sheep follow him: for they know his voice. John 10:3-4)

Do you have a puppy, a feline, or some other pet? On the off chance that you do, you realize that they get used to the sound of your voice. A few creatures can even tell where you are in the house just by tuning in for your voice. When you need to discover God, you simply need to tune in for his voice. You can hear it when you read the Bible, when you say your petitions, and when you appreciate the breeze, rain, and winged animals outside. The more you tune in for God's voice, the better you will progress toward becoming at remembering it!

The more you tune in, the more you'll hear And soon you'll know God is exceptionally close!

Day 236
The Very Best Life

(The thief cometh not, but for to steal, and to kill, and to destroy; I am come that they might have life, and that they might have it more abundantly. John 10:10)

When you have a family that affections you, companions to play with, and a delightful world to live in, you can be truly appreciative. In any case, none of those things would matter in the event that you didn't have God's adoration to finish everything off. With God in your heart, you have the absolute best life you could request: God adores you regardless, he needs to give you the best of everything, and he will watch over you for whatever is left of your life. What more would you be able to request?

God makes my life as well as can be expected be, I am so happy he watches over me!

Day 237
Safe And Happy

(I am the good shepherd: the good shepherd giveth his life for the sheep. John 10:11)

Sheep are charming, however they aren't exceptionally savvy. In the event that nobody is around to deal with them, they get lost and terrified, and they cause harm. That is the reason sheep require a shepherd to enable them to remain protected and glad. Now and then individuals are similar to sheep. We get befuddled about what we ought to do or shouldn't do. We cause terrified and we get harm. That is the reason we require Jesus. He's dependably there to secure us and demonstrate to us the correct approach. Jesus, my shepherd, causes me make the right decision. I know he'll secure me by day and by night.

Day 238
For All Time

(Jesus said unto her, I am the resurrection, and the life: he that believeth in me, though he were dead, yet shall he live: John 11:25)

On the off chance that you've at any point had a grandpa, grandmother, parent, sister, or sibling who passed on, you know it damages to have somebody you cherish leave. Be that as it may, Jesus made us a magnificent guarantee.

He said that when we put stock in him, after we pass on, we will live once more. We won't live on earth until the end of time. Be that as it may, we will live in paradise with God forever. And every one of those individuals who put stock in Jesus and kicked the bucket before us will be there as well, cheerful to see us once more.

Despite the fact that I'm tragic when friends and family leave, I'll be cheerful to see them again one day.

Day 239
When You Feel Sad

(Jesus wept. John 11:35)

Jesus was God's Son, yet he was likewise a man who felt a great deal of similar sentiments you feel. At the point when his great companion Lazarus passed on. Jesus was, extremely miserable. he was sad to the point that he cried. Despite the fact that Jesus realized that Lazarus would be in paradise one day, regardless he missed his companion and felt awful. When you're dismal, request that Jesus be with you and solace you. Keep in mind that, he knows exactly how you feel.

When I feel miserable, I know God will mind. He knows how I feel and he'll generally be there.

Day 240
Teamwork

(Let not your heart be troubled: ye believe in God, believe also in me. John 14:1)

When you are a piece of a team, you cooperate with the various colleagues to complete things. On a games team, every one of the players cooperate to win. Your family is another sort of a team. Regardless of whether it's cleaning the house or rounding the leaves up the yard, the work completes speedier if everybody cooperates. God the Father and Jesus his Son are a team as well. When you converse with God, you are conversing with Jesus, as well. When you solicit God to be a section from your life, Jesus will be as well. God the Father and his Son make the best team of all.

God is the Father, Jesus the Son. Say thanks to them for all the immense things they've done.

Day 241
Our Heavenly Home

(In my Father's house are many mansions: if it were not so, I would have told you. I go to prepare a place for you. John 14:2)

At the point when organization goes to your home, you likely need to put all your toys away and ensure your room is spotless. Presently envision Jesus preparing paradise for every one of his companions. Perhaps he's setting up an uncommon spot only for you or getting a devour of all your most loved nourishments prepared. Whatever Jesus is doing, he's ensuring that paradise will be an uncommon place – only for companions like you! Jesus is occupied in paradise today, Preparing a home I'll live in sometime in the not so distant future.

Day 242
Home, Sweet Home

(And if I go and prepare a place for you, I will come again, and receive you unto myself; that where I am, there ye may be also. John 14:3)

Jesus' companions here on earth adored him in particular. So when he disclosed to them he was leaving to backpedal to paradise, they were pitiful. In any case, he likewise disclosed to them that one day they'd all be as one again in paradise. That is Jesus guarantee to us, as well. On the off chance that you trust that Jesus is God's Son, some time or another you'll go to paradise as well. Also, you'll live with Jesus. You'll get the opportunity to converse with him, sit with him, play with him, and sing with him. You'll get the opportunity to go through everlastingly with the absolute best companion you would ever have.

In paradise, I'll see Jesus vis-à-vis, And live with him in that magnificent place – paradise, heaven.

Day 243
Just Follow Jesus

(Jesus saith unto him, I am the way, the truth, and the life: no man cometh the Father, but by me. John 14:6)

In the event that you ever think about how to get to paradise (heaven), the appropriate response is simple. Simply take after Jesus. You don't need to be particularly brilliant or okay or even great. You should simply solicit Jesus to be in control from your life. When you do, you'll be on the way to paradise. Jesus is pointing the way. We should simply take after.

Getting to heaven is simple, I know. Putting stock in Jesus is the correct approach.

Day 244
God At Work

(If ye shall ask any thing in my name, I will do it. John 14:14)

More than anything, Jesus needs individuals to love his Father. All that he said and did while he was on earth was to help us and love God. Jesus says he'll do whatever we ask, as long as it encourages individuals develop nearer to God. When you supplicate, make sure to approach Jesus for things that will help other people feel God's affection. Request that he enable you to be adoring and patient and kind. At that point prepare to watch God work!

God will give what you request in supplication. So request that he enable you to demonstrate others his care.

Day 245
For A Little While

(I will not leave you comfortless: I will come to you. John 14:18)

At the point when your mother or father leaves on an outing, it's alright to feel somewhat frightened. At the point when Jesus told his companions he was leaving for some time, they got terrified as well. However, he guaranteed them he'd be with them once more. Today he makes a similar guarantee to us. Despite the fact that we can't see Jesus strolling around on the earth any longer, we know he's with us. Also, we'll see him in paradise one day,

Jesus, you'll never allow me to sit unbothered. I anticipate your great home.

Day 246
Love And Obey

(If ye keep my commandments, ye shall abide in my love; even as I have kept my Father's commandments, and abide in his love. These things have I spoken unto you, that my joy might remain in you, and that your joy might be full. John 15:10-11)

What are some ways you indicate individuals you adore them? Do you give them much love? Or, on the other hand share your most loved toy? Or, then again spare them a seat at the table? Those are largely extraordinary approaches to demonstrate love. You can demonstrate your adoration for Jesus, as well however in an unexpected way. In spite of the fact that you can't physically give him an embrace, you can do what he requests that you do. You can tune in to your mother and father, or you can comfort a stinging companion. When you obey Jesus, that is the best "embrace" you can give him.

Since I adore Jesus, I need to comply. I'll do what he requests that I do each day.

Day 247
Who Do You Love

(This is my commandment, That ye love one another, as I have loved you. John 15:12)

Jesus requests that we cherish each other. Yet, that doesn't simply mean saying "I cherish you." Jesus needs us to truly act like we adore others the way he does. What does that sort of adoration resemble? At the point when Jesus lived on earth, he adored individuals who were benevolent and individuals who were mean.

He adored individuals who looked delightful and individuals who looked common.

He cherish rich individuals and destitute individuals. Jesus adores you since you're you. He needs you to love others a similar way.

Jesus cherishes all individuals, for a long time. I'll adore them as well, in the exceptionally same way.

Day 248
Bursting With Joy

(Hitherto have ye asked nothing in my name ask, and ye shall receive, that your joy may be full. John 16:24)

What would it be a good idea for you to implore about? When you don't know, request that God help other people see Jesus in you. That is a supplication God will dependably reply. God can enable you to demonstrate his affection, care, and thoughtfulness to others, notwithstanding when you don't feel adoring toward them. When you treat others well, you'll be loaded with a magnificent euphoria. You'll feel so stupendous, you won't have the capacity to hold it inside. You'll need to impart it to everybody around you!

When I share God's adoration with every kid and young lady, God tops me off with his magnificent euphoria (joy).

Day 249
Bumps And Bruises

(These things I have spoken in unto you, that in me ye might have peace. In the world ye shall have tribulation: but be of good cheer; I have overcome the world. John 16:33)

Have you at any point been truly terrified? Like when it began to rain and thunder outside? Or, on the other hand when you tumbled off your bicycle and knock your knees on the walkway? Once in a while life will give you knocks and wounds. In any case, Jesus can help you. He can give you mettle to get past those excruciating circumstances. Why? Since he's greater and more grounded and more noteworthy than anything on the planet. What's more, he's looking out for you!

Knocks and wounds (bumps and bruises) are a piece of life as well, But Jesus is here, looking out for you!

Day 250
Warm And Wonderful

(Thou hast made known to me the ways of life; thou shalt make me full of joy with thy countenance. Acts 2:28)

There's most likely no preferable feeling on the planet over being with somebody you truly cherish. Like when you and your father have an extraordinary evening playing in the yard. Or, on the other hand when your mother sets aside some additional opportunity to cuddle with you before sleep time. Doesn't that influence you to feel all warm and great inside? That is the way it feels to invest energy with God. Furthermore, the best thing is that God will be around for eternity!

God, it's superb to be with you. You're generally with me whatever I do.

Day 251
A Loving King

(Neither is there salvation in any other: for there is none other name under heaven given among men, whereby we must be saved. Acts 4:12)

Back in Bible circumstances there were bunches of various lords who administered heaps of various nations. On the off chance that one of those rulers needed somebody to be rebuffed, that individual was rebuffed. However, Jesus is an alternate sort of King. He's a cherishing King who needs us to be glad. What's more, he knows the most ideal path for us to be upbeat is to go through perpetually with him. Jesus is the main King who has the ability to welcome us to live with him in paradise. What a superb King!!!

Jesus is our Lord, our Savior, and King. To him our affection and compliance (obedience) we'll bring.

Day 252
Bold Words

(And now, Lord, behold their threatenings, and grant unto thy servants, that with all boldness they speak thy word. Acts 4:29)

Do you know what strength (boldness) implies? Intensity is stating or accomplishing something like you truly mean it when you know it's reality. Be that as it may, it's difficult to be intense when you're anxious about what others may state or do. Imagine a scenario in which they snicker at you or ridicule you. That is the reason Jesus' adherents requested that God enable them to discuss Jesus with strength (boldness). They needed everybody to think about Jesus' affection.

God, make me strong in all I say and do. I won't be perplexed when I discuss you!

Day 253
God's Grocery Store

(Nevertheless he left not himself without witness, in that he did good, and gave us rain from heaven, and fruitful seasons, filling our hearts with food and gladness. Acts 14:17)

Do you get a kick out of the chance to go to the market? It's amusing to push the truck down the path and select the best bananas, would it say it isn't? Be that as it may, the great things you jump at the chance to eat don't simply originate from the market. Potatoes and lettuce and corn develop in rancher's fields. Apples and pears develop on trees in a plantation. Furthermore, God's the person who sends heaps of rain and daylight to enable them all to develop. So think about the earth as God's supermarket – loaded with great things!

God gives me loads of good things to eat. The earth is brimming with a wide range of treats!

Day 254
More Than A Friend

(For in him we live, and move, and have our being; as certain also of your own poets have said, For we are also his offspring. Acts 17:28)

God does as such numerous superb things for us-he's an immaculate companion. In any case, he's far beyond that! God is our maker and defender. Without him, we wouldn't have a family or a home. We wouldn't be alive. God needs us to realize that we have a place with him. We are his youngsters. He adores us more than we can even envision!

Without God in your life, you'll be dismal and desolate. So simply give your heart to him- and to him as it were!

Day 255
Tell The World

(Then spake the Lord to Paul in the night by a vision, Be not afraid, but speak, and hold not thy peace; For I am with thee, and no man shall set on thee to hurt thee; for I have much people in this city. Acts 18:9-10)

One of Jesus' devotees was a man named Paul. Not every person loved what Paul said in regards to Jesus in light of the fact that not every person trusted Jesus was God's Son. Be that as it may, God addressed Paul in a fantasy and let him know not to be perplexed. After this, Paul kept on enlightening everybody he could concerning Jesus' affection. Today it can in any case be frightening to discuss Jesus. A few people may ridicule you. Be that as it may, God guarantees to give you the bravery to tell others the amount Jesus adores them. So why not begin today?

God, enable me to be overcome when I discuss you. I know you are with me at whatever point I do.

Day 256
Strong Kids

(I have shown you all things, how that so labouring ye ought to support the weak, and to remember the words of the Lord Jesus, how he said, It is more blessed to give than to receive. Acts 20:35)

You may be small or little in size, yet you can at present do a ton of huge things to help other people. For example, you can enable your folks to deal with your more youthful siblings and sisters. You can influence more established individuals to grin by going to a nursing home. You can deal with your pets and brighten up a stinging companion. What's restricted you can help somebody today? I may be youthful, yet there's parts I can do To help other individuals who may feel blue.

Day 257
Giving And Getting

(I have shown you all things, how that so labouring ye ought to support the weak, and how he said, It is more blessed to give than to receive. Acts 20:35)

We like getting presents so much that we here and there pass up a great opportunity for how much fun it is to give presents. When you give individuals endowments you selected, you're revealing to them the amount you adore them. You're disclosing to them that they're worth considering and recollecting. You don't need to burn through cash to give somebody a blessing that way. An embrace, a card you make yourself, or even a grin can make another person feel extraordinary.

I get a kick out of the chance to offer endowments to demonstrate that I give it a second thought. God gives me so much I simply need to share.

Day 258
Safe At Sea

(Wherefore, sirs, be of good cheer; for I believe God, that it shall be even as it was told me. Acts 27:25)

Keep in mind Paul, who was reluctant to discuss Jesus? With assistance from God, it didn't Paul long to get a huge amount of bravery. This verse is from a story where Paul was on a watercraft that was gotten in a tempest. The other individuals on the vessel were perplexed. They figured the waves may influence the pontoon to sink and they would bite the dust. Yet, Paul knew God would protect them since God had guaranteed. Paul figured out how to put stock in God with his life. Furthermore, you can as well. I can confide in God to deal with me, Just like Paul did when he was adrift.

Day 259
No Doubt

(God forbid: yea, let God be true, but every man a liar; as it is written, That thou mightest be justified in thy sayings, and mightest overcome when thou art judged. Romans 3:4)

As you get more established; you may begin to think about whether what the Bible says is truly valid. You may think about whether God truly cherishes you as much as the Bible says he does. You may think about whether he'll truly watch over you until the end of time. Paul, who composed these words, discovered that God's words are constantly valid and right. Furthermore, when the Bible says that God's words are valid, you know you can trust it.

At whatever point I think about whether God's truly there, I'll simply recall his affection and his care.

Day 260
Over And Over

(There is therefore now no condemnation to them which are in Christ Jesus, who walk not after the flesh, but after the Spirit. Romans 8:1)

Have you at any point needed to remove a toy from your younger brother or younger sister? Or, then again take a bit of gum from a store? Making the best decision all the time isn't simple particularly when you truly need something. Now and then you may settle on poor decisions, notwithstanding when you realize what you ought to do. Be that as it may, when you commit errors, you can request that Jesus excuse you. Also, guess what? He will. Not only one time, but rather again and again, in light of the fact that he cherishes you to such an extent. Jesus pardons me when I commit an error. He cherishes me regardless of what decisions I make.

Day 261
Imagine This!

(For to be carnally minded is death, but to be spiritually minded is life and peace. Romans 8:6)

Envision playing an amusement with your companions. In this popularity, everybody is caring to each other. Individuals alternate, share their toys, and say just pleasant things to each other. Nobody is permitted to be mean, notwithstanding for a moment. That sounds like an extraordinary amusement, isn't that right? When we let God's Spirit into our souls he influences us to feel so great that we need to be decent. Envision a world where everyone was that way. The world would be an exceptionally pleasant place.

God, thank you for filling my heart with your Spirit. This news is so great, I need others to hear it!

Day 262
Healthy And Happy

(And not only they, but ourselves also, which have the firstfruits of the Spirit, even we ourselves groan within ourselves, waiting for the adoption, to wit, the redemption of our body. Romans 8:23)

On the off chance that you've at any point been to a healing center, you realize that doctor's facilities are loaded with debilitated individuals. Despite the fact that individuals are more beneficial and live longer now than individuals did numerous years prior, we will even now become ill now and again. In any case, God discloses to us that paradise will be an altogether different place. There won't be any healing centers in paradise, on the grounds that there won't be any affliction! Everybody will be sound and cheerful in paradise. When we get to paradise, we'll never feel awful. We'll never become ill and we'll never be miserable.

Day 263
All For The Good

(And we know that all things work together for good to them that love God, to them who are the called according to his purpose. Romans 8:28)

Everybody has great days and awful days. One day a companion may state something that offends you. One more day you may make another companion. Whatever sort of day you're having, you can make sure that Jesus isn't recently kicking back and viewing. He's helping you learn and become through every one of the things that transpire – the great and the awful.

Despite the fact that things may happen that influence me to feel dismal,

I know Jesus encourages me to develop and be happy.

Day 264
God On Your Side

(What shall we then say to these things? If God be for us, who can be against us? Romans 8:31)

When you have a runny nose and a terrible cold, you most likely need to remain in the bed. You may begin to feel desolate, particularly in the event that you see your companions having a great time without you. You may feel frustrated about yourself as well. Be that as it may, the Bible says regardless of the possibility that you have a craving for everything is conflicting with you, God is dependably on your side. While you are getting over your icy, recall this. You'll feel better before you know it.

When I have a sore throat and a stuffy head, God's still on my side while I rest in bed.

Day 265
More Than A Conqueror

(Nay, in all these things we are more than conquerors through him that loved us. Romans 8:37)

Do you know conquering something? It intends to win out-not simply by a bit, but rather by a considerable measure. Once you've vanquished something, it can never beat you again. The Bible says that God encourages us overcome all that we experience in life. Tough circumstances won't not leave, but rather they can't beat us. They can't influence us to miss out on the considerable things God has guaranteed us.

With God close by, I can overcome all. Nothing on earth can influence me to fall.

Day 266
Together Forever

(Nor height, nor depth, nor any other creature, shall be able to separate us from the love of God, which is in Christ Jesus our Lord. Romans 8:39)

After all the affection he's demonstrated his kin more than a large number of years, do you figure God would let anything interfere with him and us? No chance! Nothing you can do will shield God from adoring you. Regardless of the possibility that you say something mean in regards to somebody, God still adores you. Regardless of the possibility that you lie about taking the last candy, God comprehends what you did, yet despite everything he adores you. Never be reluctant to converse with him, notwithstanding when you settle on poor decisions. As the Bible says nothing can isolate you from his affection. Nothing can ever take God's adoration away.

Day 267
God's Family

(And be not conformed to this world; but be ye transformed by the renewing of your mind, that ye may prove what is that good, and acceptable, and perfect, will of God. Romans 12:2)

Do your grandparents influence your most loved treat when you to visit them? Or, then again does your family recount stories after supper? Each family has its own uncommon method for getting things done. That is valid for God's family as well. When we have a place with God's family, we need to be thoughtful and wanting to others. We attempt to be persistent and delicate with each other. How might you indicate you're a piece of God's family today?

When you're in God's family, there's bounty to do, Like take after God's designs and have some good times, as well.

Day 268
My Own Special Gift

(Having then gifts differing according to the grace that is given to us, whether prophecy, let us prophesy according to the proportion of faith; Romans 12:6)

Do you ever ponder what makes you so uncommon? God says he's given each and every one of us a unique blessing – something we can do truly well. God may have made you an extremely kind individual who helps other people can rest easy. Perhaps he influenced you to calm so you could be a decent audience. On the off chance that you don't recognize what extraordinary blessing God has given you, ask your mother or father or grandparents. They'll reveal to you exactly how exceptional you truly are! What would i be able to do that is uncommon and new? Whatever it is, I'll share it with you!

Day 269
God's Plan

(Rejoicing in hope; patient in tribulation; continuing instant in prayer; Romans 12:12)

At the point when God takes a gander at you, do you know what he sees? He sees you at the present time, and he sees the future, as well. You don't comprehend what you'll resemble when you grow up, however God does. He has great gets ready for you. On the off chance that you tail him and experience the way he needs you to live, God will demonstrate to you his designs. He'll enable you to locate the correct way for your life, and he'll lead you toward the path he needs you to go. Whatever God has in store for you, you can wager it will be incredible!

I'm following God-he has enormous plans for me. I can hardly wait to find exactly what they will be!

Day 270
Be On The Lookout

(Distributing to the necessity of saints; given to hospitality. Romans 12:13)

On the off chance that you heard somebody weeping for help, you'd most likely race to perceive what wasn't right. Be that as it may, in some cases individuals who require enable cry to out in ways we can't hear. A man who's miserable may very well sit discreetly independent from anyone else, or herself. A man who's ravenous may sit tight for somebody to offer him or her nourishment. In the event that we focus on others, we can discover approaches to offer assistance.

We can converse with the pitiful individual who's sitting alone. We can impart our sustenance to somebody who doesn't have any. On the off chance that you need to help other people, simply keep your eyes open. You'll be astonished by what you see!

On the off chance that I keep my eyes open, I know I'll see Ways to help other people like Jesus causes me.

Day 271
More Than A Word

(Love worketh no ill to his neighbour; therefore love is the fulfilling of the law. Romans 13:10)

Heaps of individuals discuss love. Be that as it may, what does love mean? Love is something beyond looking for good or being decent. Love implies truly considering what others require. It implies being thoughtful, notwithstanding when others aren't benevolent to you. Love is making the wisest decision, notwithstanding when it's hard. Jesus demonstrated to us an exceptionally uncommon sort of affection when he came to earth to live with us. He was constantly kind and patient. He generally thought about the general population he met, regardless of their identity or what they resembled. How might you demonstrate Jesus' sort of adoration?

Jesus indicated love to everybody he met. He's our illustration I'll always remember.

Day 272
You've Got Power

(So that ye come behind in no gift; waiting for the coming of our Lord Jesus Christ; I Corinthians 1:7)

You definitely realize that God is the most effective being in the universe. Be that as it may, did you realize that he will impart his energy to you? You can't make stars and planets like God did, yet you can act like Jesus did. God gave you a heart and a psyche to enable you to use sound judgment. He topped you off with adoration that you can share. Furthermore, he gave you Jesus, with the goal that you could take after his words and activities. Request that God give you the ability to live for him. At that point simply watch what happens!

I realize that God will give me the ability To love and offer with others every hour.

Day 273
Surprise Party!

(But as it is written, Eye hath not seen, nor ear heard, neither have entered into the heart of man, the things which God hath prepared for them that love him. I Corinthians 2:9)

At the point when individuals design an unexpected birthday party, they make sense of what the birthday individual will need to eat, which companions they should welcome, and what beautifications would be enjoyable. They make a wide range of plans to affectionately shock the birthday individual. All things considered, God hosts an awesome enormous shock gathering made arrangements for us in paradise.

We don't realize what we'll resemble, what we'll wear, or what we'll eat. Be that as it may, it will be superior to anything we can envision. Why? Since God can hardly wait to demonstrate to us the amount he cherishes us!

When I get to paradise, a gathering I'll discover. What enjoyable to perceive what God has as a primary concern!

Day 274
Celebrate Today!

(Whether Paul, or Apollos, or Cephas, or the world, or life, or death, or things present, or things to come, all are yours; I Corinthians 3:22)

On the off chance that you ponder the future, you won't not focus on the great things God gives us every day. Notwithstanding when a day appears to be standard, it's an uncommon blessing from God. Tuning in to water stream from a spigot, following a ladybug as it flutters over the yard, or playing in the sand at the shoreline or sand box at home won't not appear to be all that energizing. Be that as it may, that water, that ladybug, and that sand are for the most part blessings from God. Also, you can appreciate them completely!

Every day is a blessing from God to me. There's such a great amount to do thus much to see.

Day 275
The Way Out

(There hath no temptation taken you but such as is common to man: but God is faithful, who will not suffer you to be tempted above that ye are able; but will with the temptation also make a way to escape, that ye may be able to bear it. I Corinthians 10:13)

When you have a craving for accomplishing something you know you shouldn't, God guarantees to enable you to discover an exit from inconvenience. On the off chance that a companion needs you to be mean to another companion, God will enable you to state no. In the event that your sibling or sister request that you tell a lie, God will enable you to be straightforward. When you feel enticed, go to God. He'll enable you to discover the exit plan. He'll enable you to make the best decision.

When I'm set out toward inconvenience and losing my direction, God causes me out-I simply need to pray.

Day 276
Gifts From God

(Now there are diversities of gifts, but the same Spirit. I Corinthians 12:4)

Have you at any point known individuals who boast about all the considerable things they can do? When you hear individuals gloat, simply recall that it's God who gave them the capacity to do those incredible things. Furthermore, God gave you exceptional capacities as well. A few people can draw truly well and others can sing delightfully. A few people can draw truly well and others can recount brilliant stories.

It doesn't make a difference what you're great at. Every one of the blessings we have are from God. Also, that is the thing that issues most.

God gave all of us something uncommon to do. I have his blessings, and others do, as well.

Day 277
Wait Your Turn

(Charity suffereth long, and is kind, charity envieth not; charity vaunteth not itself, is not puffed up, I Corinthians 13:4)

Is it ever difficult to hang tight? Here and there you need to remain in a line to get a frank at a football game when you're truly eager. Or, then again you need to sit tight for your sibling or sister to complete the process of playing with the skateboard so you can have a turn. Holding up isn't simple. You can get truly baffled. However, the Bible says that being patient and holding up is another approach to indicate love to others. So whenever you need to hold up, sing a melody, say a petition, or simply recollect this verse. And after that your turn will come quicker than you might suspect!

At times it's difficult to sit tight for my turn, But tolerance is something God needs me to learn.

Day 278
Acts Of Kindness

(Charity suffereth long, and is kind, charity envieth not; charity vaunteth not itself, is not puffed up, I Corinthians 13:4)

Has somebody at any point accomplished something pleasant for you? Perhaps your sibling shared his most loved truck. Or, on the other hand a companion drew a photo for you when you were wiped out. Accomplishing something pleasant is one approach to demonstrate others how exceptional they are. So when you adore individuals and you need them to know it, accomplish something kind for them. Set the table for your mother. Tie your sibling's or sister's shoes. Embrace your father. When you indicate others you adore them, you'll feel great as well.

When I am benevolent, I am demonstrating my adoration. The adoration that is a blessing from God up above.

Day 279
The Best Kind Of Friend

(Doth not behave itself unseemly, seeketh not her own, is not easily provoked, thinketh no evil; I Corinthians 13:5)

What sort of companion do you jump at the chance to invest energy with? That is simple the sort of companion who imparts his treat to you and who gives you a chance to ride his bicycle. It's difficult to be companions with a man who dependably needs everything to be his or her way. A decent companion considers others first. So if your companion craves playing with dolls or toy trunks when you need to do something else, attempt his/or her way. Alternate. Take turns!

In the event that you need to sit by the educator amid story time however another person arrives to start with, do whatever it takes not to sulk. Be the sort of companion who alternates and offers. At that point you'll generally have heaps of companions.

Rather than pushing so things go my direction, I'll consider first others when I need to play.

Day 280
A Big Boost

(Beareth all things, believeth all things, hopeth all things, endureth all things. I Corinthians 13:7)

What does your mother or day say when you're figuring out how to explore new territory? Perhaps, "Extraordinary attempt!" Or, "You can do it!" Or, "Awesome Job!" Their words won't not enable you to make sense of how to tie your shoes speedier or hit a baseball better; yet they do enable you to rest easy. When you adore individuals, you can demonstrate it by staying with them and empowering them. In the event that your closest companion is endeavoring to peruse or your younger sibling or sibling is figuring out how to catch their jacket, let them know you trust they can do it. You're cherishing words will give them a major lift.

When you trust others truly can do it, You'll do your best to enable them to get past it!

Day 281
Love First

(Follow AFTER charity, and desire spiritual gifts, but rather that ye may prophesy. I Corinthians 14:1)

What does your mother or day say when you're figuring out how to explore new territory? Possibly, "Extraordinary attempt!" Or, "You can do it!" Or, "Incredible Job!" Their words won't not enable you to make sense of how to tie your shoes speedier or hit a baseball better; however they do enable you to rest easy. When you adore individuals, you can demonstrate it by staying with them and empowering them. On the off chance that your closest companion is endeavoring to peruse or your younger sibling or sibling is figuring out how to catch their jacket, let them know you trust they can do it. You're adoring words will give them a major lift.

When you trust others truly can do it, You'll do your best to enable them to overcome it!

Day 282
A New Life

(For as in Adam all die, even so in Christ shall all be made alive. I Corinthians 15:22)

When somebody you cherish passes on, you feel tragic on the grounds that you'll miss that individual a considerable measure. In any case, when we have faith in Jesus, demise isn't the end for us. Some time or another we'll see each other again in paradise. That implies despite the fact that you feel miserable now, you don't need to state farewell for eternity.

You'll get the chance to join the individual you miss in paradise (heaven) sometime in the not so distant future where there is no misery or torment or tears. And afterward you can make proper acquaintance once more. Won't that be brilliant!

Day 283
An Amazing Place!

(It is sown in dishonour; it is raised in glory; it is sown in weakness; it is raised in power: I Corinthians 15:43)

Do you know any individual who utilizes a wheelchair or experiences serious difficulties seeing or hearing? Our bodies don't generally do the things we need them to do, in any event not here on earth. However, in the event that we adore God, some time or another we'll live in paradise with him, and we'll have bodies that work consummately. Envision failing to get debilitated or hurt, never breaking a bone or stubbing a toe. Indeed, even individuals who can't walk now will keep running in paradise. It will be an astounding spot!

When we get to paradise, we'll all vibe so great. Our bodies will work only the way that they should.

Day 284
Jesus Is The Answer

(For all promises of God in him are yea, and in him Amen, unto the glory of God by us. 2 Corinthians 1:20)

God made heaps of guarantees (promises) in the Old Testament. God guaranteed Noah, who constructed the ark, that he would dependably pardon individuals when they asked him to and never rebuff them with another surge.

God guaranteed ruler David that somebody from his family would lead Israel everlastingly; And, guess what?

That guarantee (promise) worked out as expected when Jesus, God's Son, came to earth. He's the ruler God guaranteed. What's more, a large portion of all, Jesus came to present to us God's pardoning. Jesus is a definitive indication of God's adoration.

Promises for you and promises for me, God's promises are valid in Jesus, you see!

Day 285
Marked For God

(Who hath also sealed us, and given the earnest of the Spirit in our hearts. 2 Corinthians 1:22)

Have you at any point composed your name on something that has a place with you-just to ensure nobody takes it? That is the thing that God improves the situation us when we reveal to him we cherish him. Since he cherishes us so much, he calls us his youngsters. What's more, he sends his Spirit to live inside each of us. By cherishing people around us, we can let everybody know we have a place with God.

I am God's child and to him I have a place. I'll demonstrate his incredible love the entire day long.

Day 286
Not-So-Good-Days

(While we look not at the things which are seen, but at the things which are not seen; for the things which are seen are temporal; but the things which which are not seen are eternal. 2 Corinthians 4:18)

Most days you feel glad when you wake up. Yet, now and again, a day just appears to begin severely. Perhaps you can't locate your most loved shirt, or you get eggs for breakfast when you truly needed flapjacks. Or, then again perhaps your sister gets distraught at you for playing with her toys, and nobody has sufficient energy to peruse you a story. On days like this, recollect God guarantees that in paradise consistently will be great. Also, you won't need to stress over things like lost shirts or not all that great breakfasts until the end of time.

On earth there are days both great and awful,
But nothing in paradise will make me sad.

Day 287
New Clothes

(For in this we groan, earnestly desiring to be clothed upon with our house which is from heaven: 2 Corinthians 5:2)

You are becoming greater and taller constantly. Before you know it, you've outgrown all your garments. Abruptly it's the ideal opportunity for your mother to take you shopping and get you some fresh out of the plastic new garments. New garments are incredible they can influence you to feel spic and span as well! The Bible says our body is similar to dress. At the point when our opportunity on earth is finished; our body will resemble old garments that we've outgrown.

What's more, when we get to paradise, we will put on new garments our fresh out of the plastic new radiant bodies! Paradise's so immaculate, I scarcely can hold up. I'll have another body, and life will be extraordinary!

Day 288
The Joy Of Giving

(Every man according as he purposeth in his heart, so let him give; not grudgingly, or of necessity; for God loveth a cheerful giver. 2 Corinthians 9:7)

Don't you simply love to get a present? you grin as you take a gander at the splendidly shaded paper and the bow. You ponder what's inside. And after that you get the opportunity to open it. What fun! However, did you realize that giving presents can be as much fun as getting them? When you give somebody an extraordinary blessing, give it with satisfaction. Furthermore, your blessing doesn't need to be wrapped. It can be something as basic as an embrace or a grin.

When you give blessings (gifts) with a heart loaded with euphoria (joy), You'll demonstrate God's adoration to every young lady and every child.

Day 289
Enough To Share

(And God is able to make all grace abound toward you; that ye, always having all sufficiency in all things, may abound to every good work; 2 Corinthians 9:8)

Do you have more than one toy? When you have a nibble, do you get more than one treat or an awesome huge apple? God will dependably ensure we have the things we require, similar to a warm place to rest and garments to wear. So when you're made a request to share what you have with another person, don't stress that there won't be sufficient left for you. God guarantees you'll generally have what you require.

I'll generally have a lot of good things to share, Whether toys to play with or garments to wear!

Day 290
God's Power In You

(And he said unto me, My grace is sufficient for thee: for my strength is made perfect in weakness. Most gladly therefore will I rather glory in my infirmities, that the power of Christ may rest upon me. 2 Corinthians 12:9)

Have you at any point seen a child who acted intense or who was continually swaggering around, attempting to awe others? You may think you must be intense, or solid, or immaculate to inspire individuals. Be that as it may, God says it's alright to be frail. God says his energy appears best in individuals who require him most. So we never need to stress over being something we're definitely not. We can act naturally and confide in God to demonstrate his energy in us! I need God, I'm not frightened to state, His power in me appears best along these lines!

Day 291
A Big, Happy Family

(For ye are all the children of God by faith in Christ Jesus. Galatians 3:26)

In the event that you have a sibling or a sister, you realize that it's a great deal of amusing to have somebody in your family you can play with, chuckle with, and share insider facts with.

In any case, did you realize that each individual who adores God is your sibling or sister as well? That implies you have siblings and sisters in China, Africa. India, and South America! God cherishes every one of his youngsters and needs us to love each other. Is it accurate to say that it isn't extraordinary to have family everywhere throughout the world?

My siblings and sisters aren't Just in my home. I can discover family wherever I wander.

Day 292
Showing Love

(For in Jesus Christ neither circumcision availeth any thing, nor uncircumcision; but faith which worketh by love. Galatians 5:6)

Individuals demonstrate their affection for God in heaps of various ways. A few people jump at the chance to be without anyone else's input and contemplate God. Other individuals get a kick out of the chance to accumulate with loved ones to sing tunes to him. A few people jump at the chance to peruse exceptional supplications in petition books. Other individuals get a kick out of the chance to disclose to God whatever they're considering. There's no set in stone approach to indicate God you cherish him. The only thing that is in any way important is that you do it! We as a whole love God in our own uncommon way, And we can demonstrate to him our affection consistently.

Day 293
Growing Good Fruit

(But the fruit of the Spirit is love, joy, peace, longsuffering, gentleness, goodness, faith, Meekness, temperance; against such there is no law. Galatians 5:22-23)

At the point when God's Spirit lives in our souls, God's adoration appears in our lives. Much the same as the natural product developing on a tree discloses to you what sort of tree it is, the great "organic product" that shows throughout your life tells individuals what sort of individual you are. When you're adoring, kind, patient, and the various things this verse discusses, you demonstrate individuals that you are a piece of God's family. That is the sort of good organic product that draws in others to God.

God, enable me to develop "organic product" so others can perceive

How a lot of your Spirit is living in me.

Day 294
A Friend In Need

(Bear ye one another's burdens, and so fulfil the law of Christ. Galatians 6:2)

In case you're playing an amusement and somebody gets harmed, you quit playing and endeavor to help that individual, isn't that right? All things considered, now and again individuals get hurt within. Those inside damages appear in your companion's tears or tragic face. At the point when companions are harmed, outwardly or within, you can demonstrate your affection by helping them.

In the event that a companion is tragic, give him or her an embrace. In the event that a companion is being singled out, remain close by.

At whatever point you do help your companions, you'll be sharing their issues recently like this verse says!

When somebody needs assistance, I can indicate them I mind By embracing or tuning in or simply being there.

Day 295
Well Done!

(Bur let every man prove his own work, and the shall he have rejoicing in himself alone, and not in another. Galatians 6:4)

When you're youthful, it appears like everybody can show improvement over you can. Your more established companions can ride bicycles, yet regardless you require preparing wheels. Your more seasoned sibling or sister can compose their name, however despite everything you require offer assistance. Despite the fact that you can't do everything more established children can do, attempt to do your absolute best at the things you can do. What's more, before you know it, you'll be sufficiently huge to do every one of those different things as well!

I can't do everything, that much is valid, But I'll do my best at the things I can do.

Day 296
Sow And Grow

(Be not deceived; God is not mocked for whatsoever a man soweth, that shall he also reap. Galatians 6:7)

In the event that you plant daisy seeds in your garden, what might develop? Daisies, obviously! The Bible discloses to us that whatever we plant in our heart is the thing that will develop in our life. So on the off chance that you fill your heart with mean considerations or awful sentiments, it will be hard for you to be the kind, cherishing individual God needs you to be. Yet, in the event that you let God fill your heart with his adoration and care, you'll have the capacity to indicate love and care to others. Give God a chance to plant great things in your heart and watch what develops!

My heart is loaded with God's awesome love and care, So I can impart love to my companions all over.

Day 297
Surprise, Surprise!

(And let us not be weary in well doing; for in due season we shall reap, if we faint not. Galatians 6:9)

Have you at any point shocked your mother or father by setting the supper table-even before being inquired? Or, then again astonished your enormous sibling by taking out the waste so he could rest later? Doing useful for others is a great deal of fun-particularly when you go past what's anticipated from you. Be that as it may, in some cases it's difficult to do great when you feel drained or grouchy yourself.

In any case, those are precisely the circumstances you have to do useful for others, since it will improve you feel as well! Accomplish something pleasant simply all of a sudden, Especially if it's not expected of you!

Day 298
Everything You Need

(Blessed be the God and Father of our Lord Jesus Christ, who hath blessed us with all spiritual blessings in heavenly places in Christ: Ephesians 1:3)

Who claims everything that is in your home? Your mother and father? In spite of the fact that they presumably purchased a large portion of the things you have, despite everything they let you eat the sustenance they purchase and live in the house they paid for. They share the things they claim since you are their kid and they adore you. Indeed, God shares all that he has with you-even extraordinary things like the wonderful world he made on the grounds that you are his kid! He gives you all that you require on the grounds that you are a piece of his brilliant family.

God imparts every one of the marvels of paradise to me. He gives extraordinary things to his entire family.

Day 299
What's Best For You

(Wherein he hath abounded toward us in all wisdom and prudence; Ephesians 1:8)

Your mother and father know you really well. They recognize what makes you glad, and they realize what makes you tragic. However, God know you shockingly better. He knows everything that is going ahead in your heart. He even knows things about you that you don't have the foggiest idea, similar to what you have to rest easy and be glad. That is the reason it's so imperative to confide in God. He'll generally deal with you, your entire long lasting. Notwithstanding when you don't comprehend what you need or need, God does. Also, he'll ensure you generally have what's best for you.

God realizes what I'm feeling where it counts in my heart. He recognized what was best for me appropriate from the begin!

Day 300
The Power Of Love

(And to know the love of Christ, which passeth knowledge, that ye might be filled with all the fulness of God. Ephesians 3:19)

Did you realize that the adoration for Jesus is so effective, it really gives us life? It's actual that bunches of individuals live without Jesus. Be that as it may, take a gander at all they're absent! They don't have the foggiest idea about that Jesus cherishes them regardless, knows every little thing about them, and excuses them notwithstanding when they accomplish something incorrectly.

Be that as it may, with Jesus in your heart, your life is brimming with magnificent things, similar to peace and bliss and satisfaction. My heart's so brimming with Jesus' affection and his energy, My life just improves and better every hour!

Day 301
More Than We Can Imagine!

(Now unto him that is able to do exceeding abundantly above all that we ask or think, according to the power that worketh in us, Ephesians 3:20)

Would you be able to consider anything that God can't do? Would he be able to move a mountain? Would he be able to quiet a tempest? Would he be able to influence the sea to part in two? The Bible says God can do every one of these things and the sky is the limit from there. It's hard for us to see exactly how effective God is. However, we can assume that God will dependably utilize his energy to help us. He can do things we can't envision. There's nothing he can't do!

On the off chance that God can move mountains and do significantly more, I can't envision what else is in store!

Day 302
Making A Friend

(With all lowliness and meekness, with longsuffering, forbearing one another in love; Ephesians 4:2)

In case you're similar to most children, you pick companions who are enjoyable to be with, who like similar things you like, and who are pleasant to you. As extraordinary as it is to have great companions, it's far superior to be a decent companion. When you are caring and delicate to others, they'll adore being your companions.

Also, when you like your companions only the way they are, they'll remain your companions for quite a while.

Having a companion appears more or less great. Be that as it may, being a companion is still even better.

Day 303
Forgiving One Another

(And be ye kind one to another, tenderhearted, forgiving one another, even as God for Christ's sake hath forgiven you. Ephesians 4:32)

Have you at any point been so frantic at somebody you simply needed to shout? At the point when your sister ruins the photo you've been chipping away at throughout the evening or your younger sibling breaks your most loved toy, it's anything but difficult to get super furious. Be that as it may, God needs us to excuse our siblings and sisters and companions and guardians notwithstanding when they make us distraught. God excuses us each time we commit an error. We simply need to ask him. Also, he needs us to do likewise for others. Whenever you're furious at somebody, request that God enable you to excuse that individual.

God, enable me to excuse my family and companions With generosity(kindness) and love that never will end.

Day 304
Favorite Gifts

(Giving thanks always for all things unto God and the Father in the name of our Lord Jesus Christ; Ephesians 5:20)

What are some of your most loved things? Do you like snowflakes? What about plumes or heaps of leaves or goldfish saltines? Every one of the things you cherish are blessings from God. From cushioned mists in the sky to rich dark earth in the ground, God gives you numerous great things to appreciate. Whenever you're getting a charge out of one of your most loved things, make certain to state, "Expresses gratitude toward God!"

Much obliged to you for snowballs and blue skies and gloves, Friendship and quills and little, cushioned cats!

Day 305
God Notices

(Knowing that whatsoever good thing any man doeth, the same shall be receive of the Lord, whether he be bond or free. Ephesians 6:8)

Once in a while the decent things we do don't get took note. You may make your bed, yet your mother or father doesn't see it. You may draw a butterfly and offer it to a companion, yet he doesn't state bless your heart. Yet, notwithstanding when others don't see the great things you do, God does. Furthermore, he'll have a superb reward sitting tight for you in paradise.

When I do great things, I realize that God sees. My reward is in paradise, recently sitting tight for me.

Day 306
Friends Are Special

(I thank my God upon every remembrance of you. Philippians 1:3)

Do you have an exceptional companion who dependably influences you to rest easy? Perhaps it's your grandmother or your neighbor or a companion from school. When you invest energy with your companion, or notwithstanding when you're simply contemplating the amount you adore that individual, say a little thank-you petition to God. And afterward tell that individual the amount you welcome him or her as well! An exceptional companion is one of the absolute best blessings God can give you.

I adore my companions, and I'll disclose to them I do, I'll likewise tell God by saying, "Much obliged!"

Day 307
God's Not Finished Yet

(Being confident of this very thing, that he which hath begun a good work in you will perform it until the day of Jesus Christ; Philippians 1:6)

It requires investment to make something truly exceptional. When you paint an excellent picture or construct a post, you need to invest a great deal of energy into it to get it without flaw. All things considered, to God you're a lovely creation. He's put a considerable measure of energy into making you without flaw as well, and he's not done yet. Every day God encourages you discover some new information. Furthermore, he encourages you develop nearer to him.

I know I'm not impeccable so I won't overlook God's dealing with me, and he's not finished yet.

Day 308
The Power To Please

(For it is God which worketh in you both to will and to do of his good pleasure. Philippians 2:13)

When you consider obeying God, you may feel like there are recently an excessive number of standards. Perhaps you figure you can't in any way, shape or form be tantamount to God needs you to be. However, God doesn't anticipate that you will be great and dutiful without anyone else's input. To begin with God places somewhere down in your heart a powerful urge to do what satisfies him. And afterward he gives all of you the power you have to love and obey him. With is incredible help, you can't lose!

God is working profound inside me, Giving me all the power I require!

Day 309
Thanks, God!

(Be careful for nothing; but in every thing by prayer and supplication with thanksgiving let your requests be made known unto God. Philippians 4:6)

God cherishes it when you disclose to him what you require. Be that as it may, he likewise adores it when you express gratitude toward him for every one of the things he improves the situation you. When you converse with God, simply ahead and enlighten him concerning your day. Disclose to him what irritated you and what went awesome. Reveal to him what you'd like him to assist you with. Yet in addition invest some energy revealing to him the amount you adore all the great things he gives you. Like daylight and guardians and companions.

Bear in mind to say thanks to him! God loves to hear every one of the things that you say, But make sure to express gratitude toward him each time that you pray.

Day 310
Recipe For A Happy Heart

(Finally, brethren, whatsoever things are true, whatsoever things are honest, whatsoever things are just, whatsoever things are pure, whatsoever things are lovely, whatsoever things are of good report; if there be any virtue, and if there be any praise, think on these things. Philippians 4:8)

On the off chance that you blend pickle juice, raisins, soil, oranges, old bread, and nutty spread together, what will you get? A major wreckage! Undoubtedly not treats! The things you combine have a major effect. The same is valid for what you put in your brain and heart. So in the event that you need your heart and brain to be loaded with goodness, you need to put great things into them. Rather than contemplating frightening things or mean things or tragic things, consider all the great things God has given you and all the adoration he has for you. That is a formula for a cheerful heart!

Thinking thoughts both great and genuine –
Makes upbeat hearts for me and you!

Day 311
Learn And Go

(Those things, which ye have both learned, and received, and heard, and seen in me, do: and the God of peace shall be with you. Philippians 4:9

Every one of the things you gain from the Bible are brilliant, yet they truly just issue on the off chance that you work on doing what you've realized. So when God says to love your neighbor, go out and help a companion. At the point when God says to comply with your folks, do your errands with a grin. At the point when God says to be benevolent to others, share your toys with your siblings and sisters. All the important things God shows us are intended to be put without hesitation. So go ahead!

The Bible is loaded with awesome approaches to demonstrate God's adoration to the majority of the general population we know.

Day 312
Strong In God

(I can do all things through Christ which strengthens me. Philippians 4:13)

God helped Moses and Abraham and David and Jonah and numerous others in the Bible. The Old Testament is brimming with their energizing stories. Regardless of what sort of inconvenience they were in, God was their ally. God gave them the quality they expected to battle wars and spare whole countries. What's more, he'll give all of you the quality you require as well. You can confide in God. He's been helping his kin until the end of time. Moses confided in God, and I can, as well. Much the same as Moses, I know God is valid!

Day 313
More Than You Need

(But my God shall supply all your need according to his riches in glory by Christ Jesus. Philippians 4:19)

At the point when the Bible says God has wealth, it doesn't imply that he has heaps of cash. It implies that he's rich with affection and influence and he utilizes his adoration and influence to give each of us exactly what we require. He won't not give you a horse or a swimming pool, yet he'll encompass you with individuals who think about you. He'll give you the guarantee of his adoration and absolution for all eternity. At the point when God deals with your necessities, you'll feel rich as well!

God's rich in affection and rich in influence – He gives me all I need every hour.

Day 314
Jesus Understands

(Who is the image of the invisible God, the firstborn of every creature; For by him were all things created, that are in heaven, and that are in earth, visible and invisible, whether they be thrones, or dominions, or principalities, or powers; all things were created by him, and for him; And he is before all things; and by him all things consist. Colossians 1:15-17)

At the point when Jesus live on earth, he wasn't only a truly pleasant man who cherished individuals. He was, and still is, God's Son. Jesus was God in a human body, a man who comprehended what it resembles to be a youngster, adolescent, and an adult. In view of Jesus, we realize that God comprehends the world and the general population in it. Jesus lived as a man, he was human like me. He knows how life on earth can be!

Day 315
No More Grudges

(Forbearing one another, and forgiving one another, if any man have a quarrel against any; even as Christ forgave you, so also do ye. Colossians 3:13)

Do you know what resentment is (Grudges)? It's clinging to the awful emotions you have about the way somebody treated you. In the event that a companion takes your toy and after two weeks you're as yet distraught at her, that is resentment. God needs you to relinquish your feelings of resentment and pardon the individuals who hurt you. In the event that you do, God will be cheerful and you will be, as well. You'll feel so much better when you dispose of your resentment!

I'll never hold feelings of spite (Grudges), it just won't do, When it's so considerably more pleasant forgiving you!

Day 316
Why Obey?

(Children, obey your parents in all things for this is wellpleasing unto the Lord. Colossians 3:20)

God needs you to comply with your folks, notwithstanding when you would prefer not to. Once in a while they request that you get dressed, yet you'd rather play. Or, on the other hand they instruct you to have your supper, yet you just need dessert. God gave you guardians so that you'd grow up solid and cheerful. At the point when your folks request that you accomplish something-Or let you know not to accomplish something-God needs you to obey them. They're dealing with you, much the same as God needs them to. My parents deal with me, much the same as they should. I need to obey them and endeavor to be great.

Day 317
With All Your Heart

(And whatsoever ye do, do it heartily, as to the Lord, and not unto men. Colossians 3:23)

When you have to tidy up your room, have you at any point pushed your stuff under the bed as opposed to putting it away? Despite the fact that having a spotless room is not the most essential thing on the planet, God needs you to put your best exertion into all that you do. Regardless of the possibility that you don't to things impeccably, you'll know in your heart that you've done as well as can be expected. Furthermore, that is all God, and your folks, request.

Whatever I do, I will put forth a strong effort, And then I'll put stock in God to deal with the rest.

Day 318
A Good Example

(And we beseech you, brethren, to know them which labour among you, and are over you in the Lord, and admonish you; And to esteem them very highly in love for their work's sake. And be peace among yourselves. 1 Thessalonians 5:12-13)

Does your grandmother love to converse with Jesus consistently? Is your more seasoned sister or sibling constantly kind to others? Individuals who live for God and demonstrate his adoration to others enable every one of us to make sure to do likewise. In case you're willing to gain from them and take after their case, they'll enable you to develop nearer to God. Furthermore, who knows? Somebody may take after your case as well! God, much obliged for the individuals who show me about you.

They enable me to love you in all that I to do.

Day 319
Be Good To Each Other

(See that none render evil for evil unto any man, but ever follow that which is good, both among yourselves, and to all men. 1 Thessalonians 5:15)

When somebody offends you, it's normal to need to hurt them back. In any case, that just leaves two individuals with hurt sentiments. Rather than harming somebody who's harmed you, have a go at accomplishing something decent for that individual rather, such as sharing a page of your shading book or requesting that him or her play get with you. You'll be shocked at how great it feels to "do good"!

When somebody I know tries to hurt me or battle, Instead I'll do great, 'cause I realize that is what's right.

Day 320
A "Thanks" Hunt

(In every thing give thanks; for this is the will of God in Christ Jesus concerning you. 1 Thessalonians 5:18)

In the event that you lost your most loved squishy toy, it would be really difficult to be grateful, wouldn't it? Be that as it may, the Bible instruct us to be appreciative, regardless. Notwithstanding when something hard happens, God can enable us to observe a remark appreciative for, Like that soft toy. Regardless of the possibility that it's gone, you could be grateful you had it for a little time. Also, you can simply be appreciative for God's solace while you're pitiful. Why not go on a "much obliged" chase every day? What can be appreciative for now?

Each morning, when I see another day, I can be grateful at work and having an effect on everything!

Day 321
A Heavenly Kid

(Faithful is he that calleth you, who also will do it. 1 Thessalonians 5:24)

God is so intense, he can have anything he needs. Be that as it may, do you know what he needs the vast majority of all? You! You're not simply something he made one day when he was exhausted. You are his unique tyke, somebody he cherishes so much that he can hardly wait for you to live with him perpetually; That's the reason he will dependably stay faithful to his commitment to watch over you, control you, ensure you, adore you, and pardon you. That is the thing that a brilliant Father improves the situation his children.

God is my Father, my guide, and my companion. He says he'll watch over me until the end.

Day 322
As Good As Can Be

(Wherefore also we pray always for you, that our God would count you worthy of this calling, and fulfill all the good pleasure of his goodness, and the work of faith with power; 2 Thessalonians 1:11)

What places you in a better than average temperament? Eating pizza with your father? Or, on the other hand playing recreations with your sibling or sister? Presently consider how you feel when you're in a truly awful temperament. Suppose it's an ideal opportunity to go to bed, however you don't feel tired. So you step your feet and yell and cry. Yet, despite everything you need to go to bed. It's substantially more pleasant to be in a decent state of mind, would it say it isn't? You can be, as well, since God guarantees to enable you to be similarly on a par with you need to be! When I make the wisest decision, my state of mind is so brilliant. I'm on a par with can be, and brimming with God's light!

Day 323
Whatever The Weather

(But the Lord is faithful, who shall stablish you, and keep you from evil. 2 Thessalonians 3:3)

Once in a while the climate is quite recently immaculate, would it say it isn't? Clear blue skies, heaps of splendid daylight, fresh fall air. Also, in some cases the climate is the polar opposite, with uproarious accidents of thunder, brilliant electrical discharges, overwhelming precipitation, and snow. In a few places there are even tornadoes, sea tempests, or quakes. In any case, regardless of how terrifying the climate may appear to be, recollect forget that God is more grounded than anything. He guarantees to ensure you, regardless!

Regardless of whether daylight and blue skies or rain noticeable all around, I'm happy God's security is all around!

Day 324
A Heart Full Of Love

(Now the end of the commandment is charity out of a pure heart, and of a good conscience, and of faith unfeigned;1 Timothy 1:5)

Have you at any point put on a show to be debilitated to get some additional consideration? Or, then again faked crying to get your direction? You can counterfeit a ton of things, yet you can't phony love. Love is something that rises from what's inside you. In the event that your heart is loaded with awful emotions or irate considerations, it's hard for adoration to turn out. In any case, when your heart is brimming with God, cherish can't resist the urge to spill out of you. So proceed let love spill out of your full heart! My heart's loaded with adoration, and I need to share it. Keep it inside? Gracious, I just couldn't bear it!

Day 325
God Uses You!

(Let no man despise thy youth; but be thou an example of the believers, in word, in conversion, in charity, in spirit, in faith, in purity. 1 Timothy 4:12)

Notwithstanding when you're pretty much little, God can do huge things through you. He can utilize the delight you feel each day to enable more seasoned individuals to feel euphoric, as well. He can utilize your fervor about the world to remind grown-ups how magnificent his creation is. Also, he can utilize your delicate heart to indicate adults what genuine love resembles. God has loads of plans for you, and prepare to be blown away. They begin at the present time!

I may be youthful, however there's parts I can do. God can utilize me in his enormous kingdom, as well.

Day 326
Long-Distance Love

(I Thank God, whom I serve from my forefathers with pure conscience, that without ceasing I have remembrance of thee in my prayers night and day; 2 Timothy 1:3)

When somebody you adore lives far away, it's not generally simple to demonstrate to them the amount you think about them. Be that as it may, a brilliant aspect regarding being a piece of God's huge family is that we can request that God give additional adoration to our loved ones. When you say your supplications today around evening time, request that God give some additional affection to your grandparents or your cousins or your auntie and uncle who live far away. Regardless of how far away they are, God's arms of adoration are sufficiently long to contact them. My loved ones may live far away, But I can in any case petition God for them consistently.

Day 327
Full Of Courage

(For God hath not given us the spirit of fear; but of power, and of love, and of a sound mind. 2 Timothy 1:7)

Do you get apprehensive when you have a go at something new? Possibly you truly need to figure out how to swim, however that profound water is still somewhat alarming. Or, on the other hand possibly you stress when your folks abandon you with a sitter for a couple of hours. When you feel terrified, request that God fill you with mettle. When you have his energy and trust in you, there's not something to fear!

When I get terrified or begin to stress, I approach God for help in a rush!

Day 328
Always Faithful

(If we believe not, yet he abideth faithful; he cannot deny himself. 2 Timothy 2:13)

Some days you feel brimming with vitality and loaded with confidence. In any case, different days you may feel feeble and tired with no confidence left! In any case, God is still with you. There's nothing you can do that will influence God to quit cherishing you and tending to you. In the event that you cherish God, you will dependably be a piece of God's family. He'll never release you.

God is dedicated, notwithstanding when I am most certainly not. I'm a piece of his family-I'm cherished a considerable measure!

Day 329
A Ready Helper

(For in that he himself hath suffered being tempted, he is able to succour them that are tempted. Hebrews 2:18)

At the point when Jesus lived on earth, he encountered similar sorts of sentiments you do. He got furious and he felt tragic. Individuals attempted to motivate him to do things he knew he shouldn't. So Jesus comprehends what it feels like to be harmed or to be enticed. When you feel terrible, or when you're pondering accomplishing something you know isn't right, converse with Jesus about it. He knows how you feel, and he's prepared to offer assistance. Simply ask him!

When I'm enticed to do what I know is wrong, I'll approach Jesus, regardless of whether it's day or night.

Day 330
Words Of Life

(For the word of God is quick, and powerful, and sharper than any two-edged sword, piercing even to the dividing asunder of soul and spirit, and of the joints and marrow, and is a discerner of the thoughts and intents of the heart. Hebrews 4:12)

Have you at any point seen how your most loved stories become animated when you read them? When you're out strolling in the forested areas, you can practically picture the animals from Where the Wild Things Are frolicking through the timberland, or Curious George swinging from the trees. The stories in the Bible wake up as well. Each time you experience the way the Bible instructs you to, you're helping individuals see that God's Word is something other than letters on a page. It's loaded with genuine power. The Bible is truly God's effective Word, Each exuberant story just holds up to be heard!

Day 331
The King Of All

(Let us therefore come boldly unto the throne of grace, that we may obtain mercy, and find grace to help in time of need. Hebrews 4:16)

Envision living in a nation that has a ruler and a ruler. Presently envision you have an inquiry or an issue. Would you simply stroll up to the intense lord and ruler and say, "Howdy, I require offer assistance"? No chance! In any case, God is the best King of all. Also, he reveals to us we can come to him whenever, with any issue. You don't need to be apprehensive about moving toward God's royal position!

I am so happy I can converse with my King. I know I can get some information about anything!

Day 332
Full Of Faith

(Let us draw near with a true heart in full assurance of faith, having our hearts sprinkled from all evil conscience, and our bodies washed with pure water. Hebrews 10:22)

The entire Bible is brimming with stories about God's affection for his kin. So when you need to converse with God, you don't have to think about whether he's distraught at you for botches you've made. What's more, you never need to think about whether he's truly tuning in to you. Why? Since God dependably cherishes you! Furthermore, he's burned through a large number of years demonstrating the amount he tends to his kin. That is the reason you can make sure he watches over you, as well! I can be sure God tends to me. He's adored his kin all through history!

Day 333
Join Together

(And let us consider one another to provoke unto love and to good works. Hebrews 10:24)

Since we're a part of God's family, we're never without anyone else. We can do a wide range of things to help each other love God and demonstrate his affection to others. In the event that you see a forlorn young lady on the play area, snatch a couple of companions and go converse with her together. in the event that you choose to enable your folks to rake leaves, ask your siblings and sisters to participate. When we cooperate, we can increase the affection we demonstrate others – and the great deeds, as well.

Why not participate with your sisters and siblings To demonstrate God's adoration together to others?

Day 334
Faith Is . . . –

(Now FAITH is the substance of things hoped for, the evidence of things not seen. Hebrews 11:1)

Faith is a word that even adults experience serious difficulties understanding. Be that as it may, the Bible verse makes it entirely clear. Faith is thinking something is valid. You have Faith that the sun will come up in the morning, or that you'll praise your birthday again this year. Since we can't see God's face or touch his hands, we need to have Faith that he is genuine. Also, much the same as the sun, God is with us consistently. You can trust it on the grounds that the Bible says it's valid!

God gives me the Faith to know he is genuine. In spite of the fact that I can't see him, It's his love I feel.

Day 335
Just Like Jesus

(Looking unto Jesus the author and finisher of our faith; who for the joy that was set before him endured the cross, despising the shame, and is set down at the right hand of the throne of God. Hebrews 12:2)

When you need to know how to treat others with love and how to take after God, envision what Jesus would do. Jesus was benevolent to everybody. He conversed with God consistently. He generally made the best choice, notwithstanding when he was enticed to foul up. When you aren't sure what to do, keep your eyes on Jesus. At that point you can love others with a similar sort of adoration Jesus has.

When I don't know what to do or to state, I'll simply watch Jesus-he'll demonstrate to me the way.

Day 336
A Friend For Life

(Let your conversation be without covetousness; and be content with such things as ye have; for he hath said, I will never leave thee, nor forsake thee. Hebrews 13:5)

Have you at any point been playing with a gathering of children when all of a sudden they all keep running off and allow you to sit unbothered, alone? That is a desolate inclination. Be that as it may, it's an inclination you'll never have with God. Regardless of how extreme things get in your life, or how awful you feel, God will never, ever abandon you. Regardless of the possibility that you neglect to chat with him for quite a while, he won't disregard you. He'll be with you consistently, from now until the finish of time. God won't abandon me-he'll generally be close. Each time I talk, I realize that he'll hear.

Day 337
A Real Helper

(So that we may boldly say, The Lord is my helper, and I will not fear what man shall do unto me. Hebrews 13:6)

Wouldn't it be cool to have a fanciful companion who could ensure nothing awful at any point transpired? Your nonexistent companion could confront any individual who attempted to hurt you, enable you to discover things when they get lost, or even give you an embrace when you're feeling terrible. Be that as it may, Jesus is far better than a fanciful companion. Jesus cherishes you and can fill you with the mettle you have to deal with anything that occurs in your life. Now that is a genuine companion, and a genuine assistant, as well!

With Jesus next to me, there's nothing to fear. Jesus' dependably with me, and He's exceptionally close!

Day 338
Jesus Never Changes

(Jesus is the same yesterday, and today, and for ever. Hebrews 13:8)

The Bible discloses to us how Jesus, who lived on the earth, love little kids. He got a kick out of the chance to go through with individuals, regardless of the possibility that they had committed huge errors. Jesus lives in paradise now, yet he hasn't changed a bit. Regardless he adores kids like you, despite everything he needs to hear about you, despite everything he needs to excuse you when you accomplish something you shouldn't. Jesus' affection for you will never show signs of change not today, not tomorrow, not ever! Jesus will remain the same, the majority of my days. He never will change his kind, cherishing ways.

Day 339
The Wise Choice

(If any of you lack wisdom, let him ask of God, that giveth to all men liberally, and upbraideth not; and it shall be given him. James 1:5)

Indeed, even at your age, you have decisions to make each day. Like regardless of whether to eat the orange in your lunch, or regardless of whether to hand over the lost glove you found on the play area. As you get more established, the decisions will wind up noticeably harder, similar to what sort of children you should play with. What's more, when you turn into a grown-up, you'll be settling on decisions about where to live or what sort of employment to take. Ordinarily you won't make certain what to do. Be that as it may, in the event that you begin approaching God for astuteness now, it'll be simpler to use sound judgment later. All things considered, God has guaranteed to give you astuteness your entire life through.

When I have an intense decision that I need to make, God encourages me to know which way I should take!

Day 340
The Best Gifts

(Every good gift and every perfect gift is from above, and cometh down from the Father of lights, with whom is no variableness, neither shadow of turning. James 1:17)

Did you give the sun a chance to sparkle on you today? Did you get a snowflake on your tongue? Did you get an embrace from your father? Each superb thing you did today is a blessing from God.

The snowflakes that liquefy on your tongue, the daylight that warms your body, and the colossal inclination you get when somebody embraces all of you originate from God. Who could request better endowments?

The greater part of the superb things that I cherish Are available from God, his blessings from paradise above.

Day 341
Take It Slow

(Wherefore, my beloved brethren, let every man be swift to hear, slow to speak, slow to wrath; For the wrath of man worketh not the righteousness of God. James 1:19-20)

When you get frantic, what do you do? Do you kick or holler or cry or mope? Those things may influence you to feel a smidgen better for a moment, yet they don't finish much. In the event that you truly need to deal with an issue, it's a ton better to discuss it. On the off chance that somebody makes you frantic, remain quiet and tell that individual how you feel. At that point tune in to what he or she needs to state. When you take after the Bible's recommendation, you'll take care of your issues quick.

When I get furious, I won't kick or frown I'll simply do my best to make sense of things.

Day 342
Words Of Wisdom

(But the wisdom that is from above is first pure, then peaceable, gentle, and easy to be entreated, full of mercy and good fruits, without partiality, and without hypocrisy. James 3:17)

Television, motion pictures, and companions would all be able to be loaded with exhortation about how to live. However, this exhortation won't generally disclose to you how God needs you to live. So how would you know what to accept? You can utilize this verse as a little test. God needs you to be benevolent, to consider others, to indicate love and absolution to individuals, and frankly. In the event that anybody instructs you to do things that aren't cherishing or kind, don't give careful consideration. Simply do what God says, and you'll end up plainly savvy.

God's way is the just a single I should take. His insight discloses to me which decisions to make!

Day 343
Seek God

(Draw nigh to God, and he will draw nigh to you. Cleanse your hands, ye sinners; and purify your hearts, ye double minded. James 4:8)

When you play find the stowaway, you need to go searching for the individual who is covering up. God doesn't escape us, yet we do need to search for him in the event that we need to discover him. Simply recall, God is dependably with us. You can feel his affection in the great morning kiss your father or mother gives you. You can hear his voice in the sound of the breeze in the trees.

You can see his magnificence in the snow, the daylight, and the huge dark night. The best part is that he's in your heart, prepared for you to discover him.

I can't see you, God, however his much I know. I see your adoration in the sun, wind, and snow!

Day 344
Humble Hearts

(Humble yourselves in the sight of the Lord, and he shall lift you up. James 4:10)

When you're modest, humble you know you require help once in a while. At the point when a humble individual peruses a story and stalls out on a word, he or she requests offer assistance. At the point when a humble individual tries to tie their shoes however can't recollect how, he or she will request offer assistance. Requesting help doesn't mean you're not savvy. It truly implies you're smart enough to know when you can't accomplish something alone. Whenever you require help, be humble and request it!

God, on the off chance that I require help with something new, I'll attempt to be unassuming and approach you!

Day 345
Perfect Answers

(Confess your faults one to another, and pray one for another, that ye may be healed. The effectual fervent prayer of a righteous man availeth much. James 5:16)

Conversing with God is something other than saying words. Supplicating is the way your heart converses with God. Furthermore, God dependably tunes in. So simply trust that God will answer your petitions, and after that watch what he does. The appropriate response may not be what you expect, but rather it will be the ideal response for you.

God tunes in to me, heart to heart. Knowing he'll answer is my most loved part!

Day 346
All Kinds Of People

(Finally, be ye all of one mind, having compassion one of another, love as brethren, be pitiful, be courteous; 1 Peter 3:8)

There are loads of various types of individuals on the planet. Simply investigate. Do you know anybody whose skin is an unexpected shading in comparison to yours or who talk an alternate dialect? Do you know any individual who can't walk or who can't do every one of the things you can do? Each individual God makes is somewhat not quite the same as each other individual God makes. Be that as it may, all individuals are adored profoundly and similarly by God. That implies you can appreciate a wide range of individuals, regardless of how extraordinary they are from you. The world's brimming with individuals so not the same as me, But we're every one of God's kids and one family!

Day 347
Little Helpers

(If any man speak, let him speak as the oracles of God; if any man minister, let him do it as the ability which God giveth; that God in all things may be glorified through Jesus Christ, to whom be praise and dominion for ever and ever. Amen. 1 Peter 4:11)

You may believe you're too young, making it impossible to truly be much help to anybody. All things considered, you presumably still need assistance with bunches of things yourself. Be that as it may, you can be more help than you might suspect! When you play with your little brother, you're helping him feel cherished. When you get yourself wearing the morning, you're helping your folks spare time. Each easily overlooked detail you improve the situation others causes them more than you know.

In spite of the fact that I am youthful, I can do parcels for others. I can help my folks, my sisters, my brothers.

Day 348
In The Blink Of An Eye

(Casting all your care upon him; for he careth for you. 1 Peter 5:7)

Wouldn't it be awesome just to flicker your eyes and make all the seemingly insignificant details that stress you leave? Simply think-no all the more being apprehensive when your mother leaves the room, not any more thinking about whether anybody will go to your birthday party. All things considered, prepare to have your mind blown. You can dispose of every one of your stresses in a matter of seconds. Simply give your issues to God and let him deal with them. You won't need to stress over a thing!

God takes my stresses so I can remain quiet. I know he holds me appropriate in his palm!

Day 349
Sharing God's Gifts

(Whereby are given unto us exceeding great and precious promises; that by these ye might be partakers of the divine nature, having escaped the corruption that is in the world through lust. 2 Peter 1:4)

Why do you assume God guarantees us to such an extent? One major reason is that he cherishes us to such an extent. However, he additionally gives us his endowments so we can be more similar to him. When you have God's adoration in your heart and you share it with others, you're accomplishing something God would do. At the point when individuals hurt you and you pardon them the way God excuses you, you're resembling God. When you are patient and kind and happy, you're sharing God's endowments. God shared all the best parts of himself with us so we could impart them to others.

I want to impart God to the general population I know, For when I give it a second thought, it's God's affection that will appear.

Day 350
Telling Time

(But, beloved, be not ignorant of this one thing, that one day is with the Lord as a thousand years, and a thousand years as one day. 2 Peter 3:8)

Did you realize that God reads a clock a great deal uniquely in contrast to we do? Since God's been alive perpetually; time in paradise isn't the same as time on earth. At the point when the Bible says God guarantees to take away all our bitterness and torment, it won't not occur tomorrow or even one week from now. It may imply that we need to hold up until the point when we live in paradise with God.

In any case, regardless of what number of our days it takes for God to stay faithful to his obligations, we can assume that he will. Numerous years to God can resemble a day. God reads a clock in his own one of a kind way!

Day 351
The Light Of The World

(This then is the message which we have heard of him, and declare unto you, that God is light, and in him is no darkness at all. 1 John 1:5)

As of now of year, it begins getting darksignificantly prior. So what do you do? You turn on a few lights. Lights can be little as little as a modest firefly or the fire from a flame on your birthday cake. A few lights are huge they can illuminate an entire room. Be that as it may, God is the greatest and brightest light there is. He is brimming with so much light and goodness that there is no dimness in him by any stretch of the imagination. God's light is so splendid, it illuminates the entire world!

In God there simply isn't anything dim. God's light is significantly more than a little start!

Day 352
A Clear Path

(But if we walk in the light, as he is in the light, we have fellowship one with another, and the blood of Jesus Christ his Son cleanseth us from all sin. 1 John 1:7)

On the off chance that you needed to pick between strolling down a dim, winding way and strolling down a brilliantly lit way where you could see precisely where you were going, which would you pick? Most likely the way you could see, correct?

When we take after God's reasonable, brilliant way, we'll discover a wide range of good things en route, similar to great companions, bunches of adoration, and God's superb absolution. What an extraordinary excursion!

When I take after God's way, I'll discover heaps of satisfaction. His way is the best for every boy and girl.

Day 353
Living For God

(But whoso keepeth his word, in him verily is the love of God perfected: hereby know we that we are in him. 1 John 2:5)

Do you ever think about whether you're making a decent showing with regards to living for God? In case you're being sufficiently caring to the new child on the piece? In case you're demonstrating enough love to your new stride parent? Indeed, don't stress. You'll never be immaculate when you live on earth. In any case, fortunately God simply needs you to put forth a valiant effort. He needs you to see how he needs you to live-and afterward to ask his assistance doing it!

Following God doesn't need to be extreme. Simply put forth a valiant effort It's truly enough!

Day 354
God's Child

(Behold, WHAT manner of love the Father hath bestowed upon us, that we should be called the sons of God; therefore the world knoweth us not, because it knew him not. 1 John 3:1)

When you are somebody's youngster, it implies you're, exceptionally unique to them. Simply ask your mother or father. There's no other individual on the planet who adores you to such an extent. That is the reason it's so magnificent to be known as an offspring of God. God's not quite recently the person who made you, he's your heavenly Father. What's more, that implies he adores you considerably more than your mother and father can!

You are God's youngster, and he truly adores you. Your mother and your father truly adore you as well!

Day 355
A New Family

(Beloved, now are we the sons of God, and it doth not yet appear what we shall be: but we know that, when he shall appear, we shall he like him; for we shall see him as he is. 1 John 3:2)

Something stunning happens when you adore God and believe him. You wind up noticeably one of God's youngsters. You additionally turn out to be a piece of an extraordinary huge group of individuals everywhere throughout the world. Furthermore, individuals from God's family adore each other regardless. They stay standing for each other, empower each other. How might you help another of God's kids today? The world is loaded with my sisters and siblings. Since we're every one of God's youngsters, we should help each other.

Day 356
Overflowing Love

(Beloved, let us love one another; for love is of God; and every one that loveth is born of God; and knoweth God. 1 John 4:7)

Have you at any point poured excessively squeeze in a container and incidentally spilled squeeze everywhere throughout the counter? All things considered, God's adoration tops off our souls a similar way. God gives us so much love that our hearts can't hold it all. It overflow to other individuals. However, it's no mischance when God's adoration overflow.

Truth be told, that is quite recently the way God arranged it. He gave every one of us that additional affection so we'd have a lot of it to share.

Give your affection a chance to spill out today! God fills my heart with so much love and care. That it's simple for me to give others a share!

Day 357
Full Of Love

(And we have known and believed the love that God hath to us. God is love; and he that dwelleth in love dwelleth in God, and God in him. 1 John 4:16)

After all the Bible verses you've perused in this book, you now know how imperative love is to God. Jesus discussed a ton of fascinating things when he lived on the earth. In any case, the thing individuals recollected most about him was the affection he gave. God has done astounding things, such as making the entire universe. Be that as it may, the most essential thing he did was send us his Son to demonstrate to us his adoration. When you cherish. When you adore God and demonstrate his adoration to others, you're carrying on with the life God needs for you. It's an existence brimming with affection. God rises to love, I realize that it's actual, So I can indicate love to others as well!

Day 358
No More Fear

(There is no fear in love; but perfect love casteth out fear; because fear hath torment. He that feareth is not made perfect in love. 1 John 4:18)

We people can fear some truly abnormal things, similar to lifts or high places or snakes or bugs. Be that as it may, the more your heart is loaded with God's adoration, the less room there is for fear. Regardless you dislike snakes or creepy crawlies, but rather you don't need to fear them. Much more essential, you don't need to fear being distant from everyone else, or of something terrible transpiring. God's adoration can take away all your dread!

At the point when God fills my heart with his awesome love, He pushes out dread with an incredible, compelling push!

Day 359
You Are Loved

(We love him, because he first loved us. 1 John 4:19)

God indicated us genuine love from the minute he made individuals. He cherished Adam so much that he gave him an accomplice Eve-so Adam wouldn't be dejected. He adored David so much that he made him an extraordinary lord, despite the fact that David committed some enormous errors. He cherished you so much that he sent his Son, Jesus, to live on earth and excuse our mix-ups. Since God initially adored us, we can love him back. What's more, we can demonstrate his great love to everybody around us, as well. God showed me that adoration is delicate and kind. It's a lesson I'll generally keep in my brain.

Day 360
From Beginning To End

(I am Alpha and Omega, the beginning and the ending, saith the Lord, which is, and which was, and which is to come, the Almighty. Revelation 1:8)

God is our magnificent Father. Furthermore, he's additionally the Creator of the universe and everything in it. He made time, he made paradise, he made perpetually; and he made you. When you gaze toward the stars, recollect where they originated from. When you see a rabbit bouncing through your yard, recall who made it. Furthermore, when you consider the future, recall who made it, and will's identity with you for all eternity!

God's been around since before time began. He'll generally be with us – we'll never be separated.

Day 361
Let Jesus In

(Behold, I stand at the door, and knock; if any man hear my voice, and open the door, I will come in to him, and will sup with him, and he with me. Revelation 3:20)

Think about your heart like a little house. Presently consider Jesus coming to visit. When he thumps on the entryway, what are you going to do? Will you be excessively caught up with, making it impossible to converse with him? Will you instruct him to return later? On Christmas we recall Jesus' birthday and the affection God indicated us by sending Jesus to live on earth.

Jesus needs to be a piece of your life today and fill you with his love.

He's making a request to come into your heart and live there for eternity. Will you give him access? On the off chance that you need to have Jesus in your heart, Letting him in is the mos ideal approach to begin.

Day 362
Angels Everywhere

(And I beheld, and I heard the voice of many angels round about the throne and the beasts and the elders; and the number of them was ten thousand times ten thousand, and thousands of thousands; Revelation 5:11)

The last book of the Bible informs us regarding a stunning dream. In this fantasy, John, a man who adored God, saw what paradise may resemble. What's more, his fantasy influences paradise to seem like a staggering spot. In John's fantasy, he saw holy messengers in paradise. However, not only a couple, or even only a couple of hundred. John heard a huge number of blessed messengers singing close to God's royal position. Would you be able to envision? What a sound that is destined to be! Furthermore, you will get the opportunity to hear it!

When I get to paradise, I'll hear heavenly attendants sing Many melodies to God, our great King.

Day 363
No More Problems

(They shall hunger no more, neither thirst any more; neither shall the sun light on them, nor any heat. Revelation 7:16)

The world we live in is an expansive place. In any case, in a few sections of the world, individuals are extremely poor. Some destitute individuals don't have enough nourishment to eat. What's more, a few people don't have great water to drink. Be that as it may, one day, each issue we have here on earth will be no more. Indeed, even the general population who had hard lives and who were debilitated or poor or hungry will have all that they require in paradise. That is a remark amped up for!

God will take every one of our issues away, When we live with him in paradise one day.

Day 364
A New World

(And I saw a new heaven and a new earth; for the first heaven and the first earth were passed away; and there was no more sea. Revelation 21:1)

In this verse John was imagining about the finish of time, when the greater part of God's kin will live respectively for eternity. John says this won't be anything like the life we have now. All that we adore will be far and away superior, and everything that causes us agony will be no more. It's difficult to envision living some place other than on earth. In any case, God guarantees that our new magnificent home will be superior to our greatest dreams.

Our life in paradise will truly be awesome. With such huge numbers of shocks, I barely can hold up!

Day 365
Streets Of Gold

(And the twelve gates were twelve pearls, every several gate was of one pearl; and the street of the city was pure gold, as it were transparent glass. Revelation 21:21)

On the off chance that you would make something that individuals would stroll on consistently, you likely wouldn't utilize the most important thing you had, okay? In any case, in John's superb dream, everything in heaven is so astounding and breathtaking that even the boulevards (streets) are made of gold. In the event that heaven has streets that lovely, simply consider what whatever is left of it will resemble!

Heaven is loaded with such a large number of extraordinary things That it's no big surprise the blessed angels all sing.

Day 366
Heavenly Days

(And there shall in no wise enter into it any thing that defileth, neither whatsoever worketh abomination, or maketh a lie; but they which are written in the Lamb's book of life. Revelation 21:27)

Would you be able to envision having an entire day when only awesome things happen! Possibly you'd wake up to a bright day, and your closest companion would be holding up outside to play with you. Or, on the other hand you'd get the chance to go to the bazaar and ride on an elephant. Or, on the other hand you'd get the opportunity to go to the sea amidst winter-and swim with a dolphin. Most days aren't loaded with that much experience, however when you get to heaven, you'll have perpetual days brimming with bliss.

God won't permit awful things into heaven. So your days will be loaded with just great circumstances and positive sentiments!

Superb circumstances are sitting tight for me. How flawless life in paradise will be!

Day 367
God's Face

(And there shall be no more curse; but the throne of God and of the Lamb shall be in it; and his servants shall serve him; And they shall see his face; and his name shall be in their foreheads. Revelation 22:3-4)

What do you think God resembles? Does he have a fluffy whiskers? It is safe to say that he is taller than your father? Would god be able to fly? Does he have enormous muscles? Nobody comprehends what God resembles, yet one day, you'll discover. When you're in paradise, a standout amongst other things you'll do is see God eye to eye. You'll get the opportunity to invest energy with him, make inquiries, and perhaps hold his hand. The best part is that you'll get the chance to tell God in person the amount you adore him. What's more, he'll reveal to you the same.

I just can hardly wait to see God's face. It's certain to be loaded with love and grace!

Day 368
Brighter Than The Sun

(And there shall be no night there; and they need no candle, neither light of the sun; for the Lord God giveth them light; and they shall reign for ever and ever. Revelation 22:5)

Would you be able to envision being so near the sun that you never, ever need to turn on a light? That is the thing that it will resemble to live with God in heaven. His adoration (love) is so capable thus splendid, it's considerably more grounded than the sun. You'll never fear the dull in heaven since it will never be dim! God's light will fill all of heaven with its glow, love and power.

God resembles the sun that sparkles down on me. His love is the light that causes me to see!

BIBLIOGRAPHY

Barnhill, C. (2001) Little Blessings: Blessing Everyday. Wheaton, Ill.: Tyndale House Publishing, Inc.

Holmes, A. (2004) Bible For Me: Quiet Times Just For Me. Nashville, TN.: Tommy Nelson, A Division of Thomas Nelson

New American Standard Bible (1998) Anaheim, CA.: Fondation Publications Inc,. (Used By Permission)

The Holy Bible (1964) The Authorized King James Version. Chicago Ill.: J.G. Ferguson Company

About The Author

The Reverend Dr. John Thomas Wylie is one who has dedicated his life to the work of God's Service, the service of others; and being a powerful witness for the Gospel of Our Lord and Savior Jesus Christ. Dr. Wylie was called into the Gospel Ministry June 1979, whereby in that same year he entered The American Baptist College of the American Baptist Theological Seminary, Nashville, Tennessee.

As a young Seminarian, he read every book available to him that would help him better his understanding of God as well as God's plan of Salvation and the Christian Faith. He made a commitment as a promising student that he would inspire others as God inspires him. He understood early in his ministry that we live in times where people question not only who God is; but whether miracles are real, whether or not man can make a change, and who the enemy is or if the enemy truly exists.

Dr. Wylie carried out his commitment to God, which has been one of excellence which led to his earning his Bachelors of Arts in Bible/Theology/ Pastoral Studies. Faithful and obedient to the call of God, he continued to matriculate in his studies earning his Masters of Ministry from Emmanuel Bible College, Nashville, Tennessee & Emmanuel Bible College, Rossville, Georgia. Still, inspired to please the Lord and do that which is well – pleasing in the Lord's sight, Dr. Wylie recently on March 2006, completed his Masters of Education degree with a concentration in Instructional Technology earned at The American Intercontinental University, Holloman Estates, Illinois. Dr. Wylie also previous to this, earned his Education Specialist Degree from Jones International University, Centennial, Colorado and his Doctorate of Theology from The Holy Trinity College and Seminary, St. Petersburg, Florida.

Dr. Wylie has served in the capacity of pastor at two congregations in Middle Tennessee and Southern Tennessee, as well as served as an Evangelistic Preacher, Teacher, Chaplain, Christian Educator, and finally a published author, writer of many great inspirational Christian Publications such as his first publication: ***"Only One God: Who Is He?" – published August 2002 via formally 1st books library (which is now AuthorHouse Book Publishers located in Bloomington, Indiana & Milton Keynes, United Kingdom)*** which caught the attention of **The Atlanta Journal Constitution Newspaper.**

Printed in the United States
By Bookmasters